Slanting the Story

Slanting the Story

The Forces That Shape the News

TRUDY LIEBERMAN

THE NEW PRESS

NEW YORK

Published in the United States by The New Press, New York, 2000
Distributed by W. W. Norton & Company, Inc., New York

LIBRARY OF CONGRESS CATALOGING-IN-PUBLICATION DATA

Lieberman, Trudy.
    Slanting the story : the forces that shape the news / by Trudy Lieberman.
    p. cm.
    Includes bibliographical references and index.
    ISBN 1-56584-577-3 (hc.)
    1. Conservatism in the press—United States.   2. Research institutes—United
States.   3. Spin doctors—United States.   I. Title.
PN4888.C598 L54   2000
070.4'4932052—dc21   99–055616

The New Press was established in 1990 as a not-for-profit alternative to the large,
commercial publishing houses currently dominating the book publishing industry.
The New Press operates in the public interest rather than for private gain,
and is committed to publishing, in innovative ways, works of educational, cultural, and
community value that are often deemed insufficiently profitable.

The New Press
450 West 41st Street, 6th Floor
New York, NY 10036

www.thenewpress.com

Printed in the United States of America

9 8 7 6 5 4 3 2 1

For Andy and Kirsten

Contents

Acknowledgments

I would like to thank The Century Foundation for research support; Matt Weiland, of The New Press, for his thoughtful editing; and Lisa Sheikh, for her leads and insights. But most of all, I want to express appreciation and gratitude to my husband and daughter, Andrew and Kirsten Eiler, for giving up precious family time and for tolerating the piles and piles of Nexis searches and paper that littered our apartment for so long.

Slanting the Story

Introduction

"Our country must have a whole new generation of conservative journalists. . . . In the long run, our nation can't survive under a big media liberal monopoly. . . . The liberals' virtual media monopoly persists in most areas, largely due to a lack of qualified conservative alternatives."
—Senator Trent Lott, fund-raising letter, March 1996

"Liberal media bias is out of control. It's indecent."
—Congressman J. C. Watts, Jr., fund-raising letter, November 1998

On November 25, 1994, a few weeks after the midterm elections propelled Newt Gingrich and his band of conservatives to the pinnacle of legislative power, conservative think tanks hit paydirt in the media. In news stories that day, The Heritage Foundation was mentioned fourteen times, the Cato Institute seven times, the American Enterprise Institute seven times, the Manhattan Institute twice, and the Competitive Enterprise Institute once. Newspapers, including big ones like the *New York Times* and the *Washington Post* and regionals like the *Palm Beach Post* and *Rocky Mountain News,* quoted think-tank

1

officials on topics ranging from taxes and prisoners to welfare and the new Congress. The *Washington Post* quoted John J. Miller, an immigration expert with the Manhattan Institute, who said it was a disservice to call noncitizens in federal prisons "immigrants," since they were "drug smugglers, not people coming here to make a better life for themselves and their families."[1] A Cato Institute official observed in the *Rocky Mountain News* that American aid doesn't actually help people in the Third World.[2] *USA Today* quoted the ever-present Norman Ornstein, the American Enterprise Institute's congressional scholar, on the role of the Senate minority leader.[3]

That morning the *New York Times* editorial page published an op-ed piece on welfare written by Myron Magnet, editor of the Manhattan Institute's *City Journal,*[4] and a *Times* news story about Germany's baby bust quoted Nicholas Eberstadt of the American Enterprise Institute.[5]

In the evening, *The MacNeil/Lehrer NewsHour* presented a program on welfare reform. Guests included Linda Chavez, representing the Manhattan Institute, and Douglas Besharov, of the American Enterprise Institute, a representative from the Ford Foundation (a safe choice for the progressive viewpoint), and Theresa Funiciello, an author and former welfare recipient who did not contribute much balance against the conservative perspective and instead seemed to bolster the conservative view. Funiciello said that what people are opposed to is the "extraordinary growth in the welfare state, which is inclusive of an enormous range of social welfare professionals who make their living off poor people. Most of the money in the welfare system never gets anywhere near poor people." That night the *NewsHour* also featured commentary by Ornstein, who gave his thoughts on the future of conservatism.[6]

All in all, it was a very good showing for conservatives, who claim they are hard-pressed to get their views into the mainstream media. In their fund-raising letters, conservatives like Trent Lott and J. C. Watts continue to deplore the liberal hegemony over the media, but in reality, the right's viewpoint is pervasive and ubiquitous.

How the right wing has come to dominate public policy debates is one of the most significant political stories of the last two decades. The right-wing success stems largely from a variety of aggressive strategies used by well-financed think tanks and policy institutes to influence the media's coverage of political and economic issues. The effectiveness of groups such as the Manhattan Institute, the Capital Research Center, the National Taxpayers Union, The Heritage Foundation, the Cato Institute, the Competitive Enterprise Institute, Citizens for a Sound Economy, and the Washington Legal Foundation (whose activities are detailed in this book) has sometimes resulted in misleading and one-sided reporting that has given the electorate a distorted view of many important issues.

Those organizations have seized upon weaknesses and problems of government programs and agencies, have attacked other organizations that stand in their way, and have successfully persuaded the media to see the solutions they want to impose as the only reasonable and feasible ones to society's problems. The result has been little or no discussion of alternatives, such as raising revenues to adequately fund Medicare, increasing the age of eligibility for early Social Security benefits, or more adequately funding the FDA to speed up drug approvals. "The reason there's no liberal Rush Limbaugh or a liberal National Empowerment Television is that the American people don't want to buy liberal products," maintains Dan Mitchell, a senior fellow at The Heritage Foundation.[7] Is it that the public doesn't want to buy them or that none are offered for sale, leaving the public with little choice?

Backed by huge sums of money from a handful of ideologically grounded foundations, right-wing think tanks operating in the states and in the national political arena have become idea peddlers extraordinaire, every bit as skillful as the sellers of toothpaste and detergent. To further their agendas, they have marketed the flat tax, medical savings accounts, Medicare reform, privatization of Social Security, and school vouchers in much the same way Procter and Gamble sells Crest. "The sophisticated ability to relate ideology to constituencies is what counts," explained William J. Baroody, Jr., former president of the American Enterprise Institute. "We pay as much attention to dissemination of product as to the content."[8] Ideas once considered the crank notions of right-wing ideologues have become law—medical savings accounts and restrictions on lawsuits for securities fraud, to take just two examples. Indeed, says Jeanette Goodman, executive vice president of the National Center for Policy Analysis (the group that brought medical savings accounts from the germ of an idea to a viable insurance product), selling ideas is no different from marketing in a for-profit company. One hit cannot make a difference, she points out. The same clear, concise message must come from every direction.[9]

And it does. Through newsletters filled with tidbits for talk shows, weighty studies and surveys, luncheons where ideas are floated over plates of chicken and vegetables, and spokespersons given friendly hearings by reporters, these groups have spread their messages to opinion leaders and to men and women on the street.

While groups on the left sometimes use the same techniques, the right has used them more effectively, and increasingly reporters are relying on them. By embracing the right-wing spin, giving it independent credibility, and spreading its messages uncritically, the press has become a silent partner, and the public is none the wiser. Says one TV journalist who asked not to be named: "They [right-wing groups] understand the propaganda potential. Viewers are confused about what's hard news and out-and-out propaganda. They can't tell the difference between Paul Weyrich [president of the conservative Free Congress Foundation] and Dan Rather."

If viewers, readers, and listeners are so confused, that bodes poorly for the media as an essential ingredient of American democracy. Ben Bagdikian, the press critic and former dean of the Graduate School of Journalism at the University of California, Berkeley, put it this way: "What gets reported enters the public agenda. What is not reported may not be lost forever, but it may be lost at a time when it is most needed."[10]

Foundations controlled by Pittsburgh philanthropist Richard Mellon Scaife, and the Olin, Bradley, Smith Richardson, McKenna, Koch, Earhart, and Lambe foundations—as well as a handful of less well known but influential organizations—are shaping American thinking. A study by the National Committee for Responsive Philanthropy found that between 1992 and 1994, twelve conservative foundations with combined assets of more than $1 billion targeted $210 million to think tanks and advocacy groups to support conservative programs and objectives. Those groups in turn have sold their ideas to the media. Specifically, those foundations gave $9.3 million to state-based think tanks and advocacy groups, $10.5 million to conservative, pro-market law firms and legal projects, and $16.3 million to support media watchdog groups, alternative media outlets, and public television and radio for issue-oriented public affairs or news reporting.[11]

The sums available from some of these foundations are significant. Take, for instance, the Milwaukee-based Lynde and Harry Bradley Foundation, whose money was derived from the manufacturing of motor controls. In 1997, the Bradley foundation gave these organizations the following amounts just for public and government-affairs programs:[12]

- *American Enterprise Institute* $810,000 for fellowships, lecture series, and foreign and defense policy studies program
- *American Spectator Educational Foundation* $127,500 for operating support, special projects, and dinner discussion meetings
- *Cato Institute* $75,000 for economic, regulatory, and tax policy studies
- *Citizens for a Sound Economy* $25,000 for general operating support
- *Competitive Enterprise Institute* $40,000 for "death by regulation" project
- *Educational Broadcasting Corporation* $100,000 for Think Tank program with Ben Wattenberg
- *Ethics and Policy Center* $325,000 for general operating support and senior fellow
- *Free Congress Research and Education Foundation* $425,000

for programming for National Empowerment Television and general operating support

- *The Heritage Foundation* $825,000 for domestic policy studies, Bradley fellows, a state relations department and a senior fellow in Southeast Asian studies
- *Hudson Institute* $250,000 for a welfare policy center
- *Manhattan Institute* $150,000 for the Center for Civic Innovation and $18,875 for a project on congregational mobilization for community transformation
- *National Center for Policy Analysis* $100,000 for research on welfare reform
- *Reason Foundation* $75,000 for general operating support
- *US Term Limits Foundation* $25,000 for general operating support

Add these sums to similar amounts given by other foundations, wealthy individuals, and corporations, and it's not hard to see the vast resources the right-wing network has at its disposal. The National Committee for Responsive Philanthropy found that in 1996 the top twenty conservative think tanks spent $158 million, most of it provided by foundations and corporations. The committee estimates that by 2000, those think tanks will have spent about $1 billion to further their strategic goals for U.S. policy.[13]

Does the public know where the ideas come from and who pays to put them on the agenda? Ask anyone why health reform failed in 1994, and fingers invariably point to a public unwilling to support a government-run program. While the infamous "Harry and Louise" commercials sponsored by the insurance industry became the symbol, it was really behind-the-scenes work by right-wing think tanks that doomed efforts at reform. Talk-show hosts and direct-mail campaigns by conservative groups fueled the ultimate scare-story that turned the public against reform—the fostered threat that people would not be able to choose their own doctor. "Some say the talk-show hosts made the biggest difference," says Jeanette Goodman. "As we saw a new issue or a new idea, we immediately addressed it. It was the most important thing for talk shows because they got materials they could feed in at a time when people were interested in what it all meant."[14] Lisa McGiffert, an advocate in Consumers Union's regional office in Austin, Texas, recalled that during a radio tour in early 1994, radio hosts all seemed to ask the same questions about doctors going to jail.[15] They apparently had gotten the question from the same source. "Heritage was instrumental in stopping the Clinton plan," says Cheryl Rubin, director of public relations at Heritage.[16] The National Center and Heritage properly claim credit for their less-than-visible accomplishments, which are a true measure of their effectiveness. "If you're effective in your advocacy work, journalists or anyone else are not aware of it," says Michael Pertschuk, co-director of the Advocacy Institute.[17]

Right-wing think tanks have found a congenial home for their messages in today's simplified journalism. Perhaps because the news business has changed so radically, groups like Heritage, Cato, and Citizens for a Sound Economy can now help define the news, and influence and shape public opinion. During a radio show in 1994 that dissected how right-wing organizations like Floyd Brown's Citizens United fed the press tidbits about Clinton's Whitewater real estate deal, *Boston Globe* reporter John Aloysius Farrell made an astonishing comment. "Floyd Brown is the media now," he declared.[18]

Conservative groups have learned to boil down their messages to fit the new model of soundbite journalism, leaving the details for the weighty studies and policy analyses disseminated in more elite venues.

Media emphasis on soundbites, anecdotal journalism, and headline services opens the door to organizations with highly partisan motives and specific narrow agendas to get on the air or in print, especially if what they have to say is titillating or outrageous. Mark Weaver, a news reporter at WMAL-AM in Washington D.C., was blunt: "Our news director says, 'I don't care what story you put on the air, but it better be interesting.' It may be ridiculous, funny, anything that gets people's attention. That's what makes money."

Weaver amplified his station's thinking for attendees at a seminar on how to manage the media for grassroots community groups sponsored a few years ago by the Free Congress Foundation. "Radio-station news departments are designed to attract and hold more audience, which in turn generates more profit, not necessarily to impart 'important' information," Weaver told his listeners. "Radio news has become a headline service. We want as many as we can get. We want them bam, bam, bam. The more stories you have, the more you cram in, the more the perception that the audience is being informed."[19]

Newspapers, too, are making stories shorter, hoping they will be more palatable to readers. When the *Buffalo News* redesigned its front page to include only three stories running about 250 to 500 words apiece, it bought radio spots to promote the change: "You can get the facts without straining your brain."[20] Consultants for the *Winston-Salem Journal* suggested that front-page stories should be six inches or less, and that a reporter should use a press release and/or one or two "cooperative sources," take no more than 0.9 hours to do each story, and produce forty such stories in a week.[21] Right-wing groups stand ready as cooperative sources to fill the abbreviated news holes.

Shorter stories inevitably mean less context and less analysis to help readers or listeners understand what's really at stake. The new-model journalism is tailor-made for the simplistic, even alarmist, messages preached by the right wing. It's easy to headline the notion that Social Security is going bankrupt and won't be around thirty years from now. The left has yet to figure out how to communicate the message that it will be. Does it take more ink or time to tell a fuller story, or is it that the left has not learned to effectively bullet-point its ideas? Or is the left unsure of its message?

At the same time, the normal constraints of the old journalistic model make it difficult to promote a reasoned dialogue on political issues in this era of idea marketing and ideological drumbeating. Dane Smith, a political reporter for the *Minneapolis Star-Tribune*, explained the futility of trying to counter the constant repetition of the right wing's messages. "There's only so far you can go in the news columns in flat-out contradicting or confirming so-called spin," he said. "It's the nature of the beast. You can't run the same story every day. It's just not what we do."[22] At least that's not what the media does unless the topic involves glamour, sex, or scandal. Monica had more cachet as a daily news story than Medicare did.

When I first began this project some five years ago, I assumed that the mainstream media were relying on right-wing groups for "balance" quotes and spokespersons "for the other side."

Instead, I found an influence penetrating far beyond the occasional quote for balance. Conservative organizations are designing the agenda, and other groups—liberal, progressive, and in-between—are called for the occasional balance quote.

This book demonstrates how, with help from the mainstream media, right-wing think tanks and organizations have discredited their opponents, moved their ideas to the front of the national agenda, dominated the debate, and engineered big changes in public policy. They have cleverly used the media, sometimes with far-reaching consequences.

I hope journalists will learn from those examples and begin to apply to interest groups (and the corporations and foundations that fund them) the same skepticism and suspicion they now heap on politicians and government officials. The media must begin to examine the "products" these groups are selling, scrutinizing both the sales claims and the consequences of "buying" them.

In 1981, the *Columbia Journalism Review* published an article detailing the many activities of Richard Mellon Scaife. That story concluded: "Scaife has helped to create an illusion of diversity where none exists. The result could be an increasing number of one-sided debates in which the challengers are far outnumbered, if indeed they are heard from at all."[23] At that time, Scaife was a new phenomenon and The Heritage Foundation, which he was funding, was a relative neophyte in the political landscape. In the past nineteen years, Scaife, Heritage, and similar organizations have come of age. Indeed, debate *has* become one-sided. The implications for the future of American democracy are profound.

I

The Right Wing Meets the Press

"As congenital amateurs our quest for truth consists in stirring up the experts, and forcing them to answer any heresy that has the accent of conviction. In such a debate we can often judge who has won the dialectical victory, but we are virtually defenseless against a false premise that none of the debaters has challenged, or a neglected aspect that none of them has brought into the argument."
— Walter Lippmann, *Public Opinion* (1922)

Using strategies that have included courting the press, attacking the "liberal" media, relentlessly repeating their main points throughout the media, and amassing the wherewithal to strike back quickly, dozens of right-wing organizations have shifted public opinion in recent years. They have given respectability to ideas and solutions that were considered impossible only a few years earlier.

Through sheer perseverance and an unrelenting commitment to ideology, right-wing organizations have successfully used the press to further their agenda of laissez-faire economics, deregulation, lower taxes, redistributing resources from poor to rich, privatizing everything from schools to street cleaning, and—above all—delegitimizing government. As Dan Mitchell, a senior fellow at The Heritage Foundation, explained the goals of his organization: "We want cuts in taxes, spending, and regulation. Our clear, overriding objective is to reduce the burden, size, scope, and cost of the federal government."[1] In recent years, the media—both major and minor outlets—have widely trumpeted those goals.

John Cooper, former president of the James Madison Institute, a state think tank that advances public policy by emphasizing limited government, free enterprise, individual rights, and a return to personal responsibility, succinctly spelled out the prescription for achieving these objectives in an article appearing in one of the organization's publications, *The Madisonian Journal*. He declared that state think tanks believe: "Social change will occur when the agents of change have accomplished two related tasks: effectively mobilizing mass public opinion and effectively neutralizing elite public opinion."

Cooper argued that elite public opinion is deeply entrenched; that "the policy presuppositions of bureaucrats, politicians, academicians, media leaders, and top corporate management is by definition resistant to change" but that mass public opinion "is often diffuse and targeted to specific issues in isolation from other issues. Further, ordinary people will generally mobilize for fundamental change only after suffering a long series of provocations."

"To neutralize resistance to change that comes naturally to elites," Cooper said, "think thanks publish sober, well-reasoned academic studies that are read by a few thousand people in a given state." "If read by the key opinion-molding elites, these publications can neutralize opposition and create

14

the 'psychic space' for new ideas to survive," he argued. Cooper recommended op-eds in newspapers and on talk radio, public service announcements, mass mailings, and rallies to move the public to new ideas and mobilize mass public opinion.[2]

Conservative think tanks are doing all of these things.

Ralph Nader and the Right

In many ways, the rise of the right-wing think tanks is a reaction to the success of the consumer, environmental, and public interest movements of the 1960s and 1970s. To understand how conservative groups have influenced public thinking over the last twenty years, it is instructive to look at how far the other side as represented by Ralph Nader and his progeny has fallen in importance to public discourse. Nader's organizations declined largely because they lacked a sharp ideological focus. In their heyday, they attacked problems on an episodic basis—the poorly designed gas tank on GM pickups, too much fat in Chinese food, inadequate labeling on frozen orange juice—and they proposed specific legislation to fix them, acting as lobbyists for the public.

Sometimes Nader's groups succeeded; sometimes they didn't. When they won, as they did with environmental and auto safety legislation, the Flammable Fabrics Act, the Truth-in-Lending and Truth-in-Packaging laws, the Fair Credit Billing Act, and the Fair Credit Reporting Act, new regulations were signed into law. But when they lost, as they did with federal standards for no-fault auto insurance or with the establishment of a permanent federal agency for consumer affairs, those issues disappeared. The Nader machine had neither the money, energy, nor ideological commitment to promote and advocate their objectives over the long haul. Despite their many successes, they never built a movement to sustain their issues, and over the years their work took on a stale quality and smug elitism that made them less credible and less effective.

As the public's advocate, Nader's goal was to balance the public interest with the business community's historic control of government, trying to change the relationship between government officials and corporate America. But Nader avoided attacking the fundamentals of free enterprise, instead striking only at its periphery. A nip here, a tuck there, and government could work better for ordinary folks who did not have the clout to force their representatives to act on behalf of their economic interests.

Nader never won the broad philosophical argument. Nader organizations cultivated Washington insiders, but when key legislative committees changed hands, their friends were gone. The right has inside contacts, too, but its advocacy strategy permeates far beyond the Beltway. Larry Mone, president of the Manhattan Institute (one of the most visible and effective right-wing think tanks), drew a distinction between his organization and Nader's. "We're not just about creating legislation but about changing public opinion. It takes a long time for ideas to become part of peoples' perceptions."[3]

Conservative think tanks emerged in the 1970s and 1980s, in part as a response to Nader's attack on business. In a memorandum written to the U.S. Chamber of Commerce, shortly before he was appointed to the Supreme Court, Justice Lewis Powell noted: "Perhaps the single most effective antagonist of American business is Ralph Nader who—thanks largely to the media—has become a legend in his own time and an idol of millions of Americans." Powell's strongly-worded memo exhorted business to fight back. "The overriding first need is for businessmen to recognize that the ultimate issue may be survival—survival of what we call the free enterprise system, and all that this means for the strength and prosperity of America and the freedom of our people." Powell charged that business had ignored the problem and he urged "careful long-range planning," and "consistency of action over an indefinite period of years" to reverse what he saw as a dangerous trend.[4] Twenty years later, conservative think tanks are well on their way to winning the broad philosophical argument. Their ideology fits with prevailing political and economic thought— the privileged position of business, as Yale economist Charles Lindblom articulated it two decades ago.[5] They have patience, stamina, and financial resources to pursue long-range goals, and they've won over the media.

Ironically, the blueprint for the right wing's media strategy sprang from the Nader organizations, which skillfully used the press to build support for legislative changes they were seeking. "Ralph was enormously strategic in approaching the media and how to use it," recalled Michael Pertschuk, co-director of the Advocacy Institute, who worked for the key Senate Commerce committee when Nader was winning his legislative victories. "Ralph talked about the media as a resource, not an enemy or friend. Watching him was a learning experience in how issues were framed to shape the outcome. In talking about auto safety, it wasn't the nut behind the wheel who was at fault, but the nuts and bolts of the automobile itself."[6] Nader helped the press frame their stories as a match

17

between David and Goliath—the helpless consumer versus the special interests of big corporations.

The right has turned media framing upside down, and has seized the language from the Nader era. While Nader framed issues as the larger interests of the public pitted against the narrow interests of big corporations, right-wing think tanks have turned this idea on its head. Through the media, right-wing think tanks have succeeded in portraying as special interests organized labor, consumer groups, environmental activists, trial lawyers, and advocates for children and the elderly—any group whose agenda is contrary to that of corporations or to the ideological interests of right-wing think tanks. Take, for example, one of the endnotes published by the Competitive Enterprise Institute (CEI) in one of its newsletters in 1995. It noted that CEI and others had pointed out the "fatal consequences of 'drug lag' and the Food and Drug Administration's 'deadly overcaution.'" CEI said that "special interest groups are marshalling to defend the FDA's choke hold on new pharmaceuticals and medical devices" and claimed that such special-interest groups "approve of the FDA's snail-like approval process that keeps potentially lifesaving innovations out of the hands of those who could benefit from them." And what special interest was CEI targeting? None other than Dr. Sidney Wolfe, who runs the Nader-affiliated Public Citizen Health Research Group.[7]

Journalists, too, have reframed the conversation. When assaults on programs for the poor and disadvantaged by the Reagan administration moved into a quiescent state, the media did not report that a lull occurred because Reagan's ideas would hurt people. They framed their stories in terms of special-interest politics played by labor unions and AARP that put the brakes on Reagan proposals to dismantle various programs. Reese Cleghorn, dean of the College of Journalism at the University of Maryland, noted in the December 1994 issue of the *American Journalism Review* that for more than a decade journalists have been shifting to the right in the language they use. "Journalists' ideology of 'objectivity,' a splendid aspiration if you know you can't achieve it, has made them captives of other people's ideology. If a news person is 'neutral,' that means in the center. If the center is to the right, so is the language of the journalist," Cleghorn wrote. He added that journalists now avoid using such "hot" words as "radical," "arch-conservative," and "reactionary" in their stories. Right-wing radicals are called "conservatives" and centrists have become "liberals." What is a real liberal? Cleghorn speculated that "nobody knows anymore, except maybe Rush and Newt. They call them Socialists or counterculturists."[8]

Cokie Roberts had one answer in the fall of 1996 shortly before the November elections. On *This Week with David Brinkley,* she said that if the public votes for a Democratic Congress "they have reason to fear they will have the extreme left." When moderator Sam Donaldson asked Roberts for her personal view, she said, "If you do look at the list of people who would be in line to take over Committee chairs, it's not a very moderate group."[9] That group included Rep. John Dingell, who has close ties to General Motors and is a staunch opponent of gun control, which allies him with one of the pet causes of the right, and Rep. Charles Rangel, who has supported targeted capital gains cuts to help economically depressed areas and has said his views "were very much like Bob Dole's views before he ran for President."[10] When Donaldson asked Roberts whether it was her idea that these congressmen were on the "extreme left," she replied that the characterization was what other people thought. Which people, she didn't say.[11]

Conservative think tanks have moved beyond framing and have come to use the media as both a friend and a foe to further their objectives. They have become masters at cultivating the press, but are just as quick to charge "liberal bias" when the media they've so carefully pampered do not stick to the conservative line.

Courting the Press

While courting the press is common among all types of political organizations, few have done so with more diligence and élan than the right-wing Manhattan Institute, which has strongly influenced New York City's political agenda. "You can't treat the job as a PR operation," says Larry Mone. "You invite the press in on a regular basis. You get a good author with something to say, and over time journalists' skepticism wears down, and you build a relationship—a mutual trust."[12]

The Manhattan Institute regularly invites reporters from such publications as the *New York Times,* the *Wall Street Journal,* and *The New Yorker* to luncheons at the Harvard Club, where reporters mingle over cocktails with conservative elites. The luncheons in the Club's red dining rooms—with its portraits of Harvard luminaries on the walls—are short and informative, and exude an air of importance. Featured speakers have been authors such as Dinesh D'Souza, David Gelernter, and Robert Wright.

Books are the core of the Manhattan Institute's communication strategy. (The think tank avoids newsletters, although it does send out short memos from time to time. It also avoids debates—"too theatrical, too institutional," Mone says.) The Institute, like most think tanks, prefers to publish its books with big-name publishers—not academic presses—so a book has a better chance of being reviewed, and the ideas it advances receive a wider hearing.[13] In the late 1980s, the Manhattan Institute supported *Liability: The Legal Revolution and Its Consequences,* a book by one of its current senior fellows, Peter W. Huber. It supported another book on tort reform, *The Litigation Explosion: What Happened When America Unleashed the Lawsuit,* by senior fellow Walter K. Olson, published in 1991. Both books helped spark the current wave of anti-lawyer sentiment throughout the country and enhanced the right wing's continued attack on the trial bar. When the Republicans captured the House in 1994, tort reform emerged as a hotly debated issue, and in 1996, legislation that would have limited manufacturers' liability for defective products passed both houses of Congress. The bill, later vetoed, would have dramatically changed the rights people now have to hold manufacturers accountable for harmful products. (Clinton eventually signed a bill that restricted lawsuits involving securities fraud.)

The Manhattan Institute became a persuasive force in the debate. "Wally and Peter created an institutional framework for reform. We had drifted into income redistribution through the tort system rather than through the tax system," Mone said. "Tort reform was invisible to the public."[14] The Institute's tort-reform gurus advised congressional staffs and were an important source for reporters doing stories about lawyers and litigation. A Nexis search shows that officials from the Manhattan Institute were quoted often in news stories discussing tort reform. One of the most prominent journalists to give tort reform a boost was ABC's *20/20* correspondent John Stossel, who hosted a special program in early January 1996, when the tort-reform debate was raging and Congress was about to return from Christmas recess. After the special, called "The Trouble with Lawyers," aired, the Manhattan Institute reported to its friends and supporters in one of its periodic memoranda that senior fellows Olson and Huber "were heavily involved in helping John shape the broadcast."[15]

The tone of the broadcast was clearly and emphatically anti-lawyer and echoed themes advanced by the Manhattan Institute. Stossel questioned whether the country can afford the high cost of lawyers and then set the premise of the show: "Like armies, lawyers can be horribly destructive, harmful to innovation, to our good will toward one another, our freedom to make choices. I haven't even mentioned what they cost . . . American laws encourage us to use armies." He concluded: "Americans file about 90 million suits a year. Wouldn't we be better off if we just solved more of our conflicts without lawyers?"[16] Stossel took his ideas to the editorial pages of the *Wall Street Journal*, where he contributed an op-ed on the same day the ABC program aired. The story box identifying Stossel promoted his TV special.[17]

Tort reform is unfinished business for conservatives, who want to restrict the ability of individuals to file lawsuits against corporations whose products injure them. Emblematic of the right wing's ability to keep an issue alive until it achieves its goals, the Manhattan Institute has continued its activities. Olson took tort reform in a new direction with his book *The Excuse Factory: How Employment Law Is Paralyzing the American*

Workplace, published in 1997. He continued to make speeches and media appearances. In 1998, the Institute hosted dinners for judges around the country to acquaint them with the issues.[18]

Through the activities of its new Center for Legal Policy Reform, it hammers away at tort reform. In January 1999, 180 people, ranging from the wife of New York's governor to representatives of investment firms, attended a luncheon seminar billed as "A Fresh Look at Litigation Reform in America." The goal was to help "build a broad consensus for reform." Speakers included Olson and Huber, former U.S. Attorney General Richard Thornburgh, and John Stossel, who remarked: "Lawyers will take all of our time, all of our money, and all our freedom."[19] In promoting Stossel, the Institute said he "has done more than anyone in the media to bring national attention to abuses in the court."[20]

Clubbing the Press

Since the days when Spiro Agnew attacked the Eastern establishment media for their positions on civil rights and the Vietnam War, the "liberal" press has been a favorite target for conservatives who believe their views have not gotten a fair shake. One needs only to look at the constant stream of fundraising solicitations from conservative politicians and right-wing organizations to see what a convenient hook the allegedly liberal press has become for raising money. Under attack, the media have moved closer to the right, and conservative positions have come to dominate political discourse in the press, creating, if anything, a conservative bias. Tim Graham, director of media analysis for the Media Research

Center, told the *National Journal* in 1996, "Certainly it is harder today to lament an exclusion of conservative ideas" in the press.[21]

Right-wing foundations support four media monitoring organizations: Accuracy in Media, the Center for Media and Public Affairs, the Center for the Study of Popular Culture, and the Media Research Center. These organizations have the task of making sure that the media reflect conservative positions. These groups monitor what Americans see, hear, and read. They are quoted frequently and forcefully on a variety of topics.

Progressives can claim only one media monitoring group, Fairness & Accuracy In Reporting (FAIR), which suffers from a chronic lack of foundation support and low visibility and acceptance in the mainstream media. Its $1 million budget is about one-third that of the syndicated column written by the Media Research Center's Brent Bozell, which has been around "more than seven years," according to the Center's marketing director Bonnie Goff, and appears in such publications as the *Washington Times* and the *New York Post*.[22] FAIR has never been able to generate much media enthusiasm for a column by its executive director, Jeff Cohen. "Jeff wasn't getting a lot of acceptance for it," said FAIR's Jim Naureckas, who edits its magazine *Extra*. "It was in a handful of medium-size newspapers. There was not a commitment on the part of op-ed editors to present a full range of the political spectrum."[23]

Indeed, it is Bozell's Media Research Center that stands out as the right's preeminent media cop. Bozell is a Republican operative with credentials earned in George Bush's 1988 presidential campaign. The nephew of William F. Buckley, he headed the Conservative Victory Committee that year. He is also connected to the Political Club for Growth, a network of conservative and libertarian activists and groups sympathetic to cutting taxes and shrinking government.

What Bozell and others perceive as liberal bias often means presenting information about government help for the poor, the homeless, the weak, and so on—information that conflicts with the objectives of the right. Tim Graham explained that ABC was once "the worst" in its approach to stories. He said that the Center had seen on ABC what he called "a repeated stream of stories on victims of spending cuts. . . . We don't see victims of tax hikes."[24]

The right defines liberal bias as giving short shrift to conservative solutions to a problem or discussing a flaw in the conservative approach. In the conservative lexicon, bias doesn't necessarily mean prejudice, but simply a point of view or the dissemination of information that organizations, such as Bozell's, would rather the media ignore. Bias can also mean information Bozell's group wants presented that the press may leave out of its reports.

To help identify and eliminate what the right perceives as bias, the Media Research Center has published several newsletters over the years, which have been distributed free to the press. *MediaNomics,* which tracked how the press covers economic issues, began in the early 1990s as a product of the Center's Free Enterprise & Media Institute dedicated to "educating the media about free enterprise." It was funded in part with a $15,000 grant from the JM Foundation and a $100,000 grant from the Grover Hermann Foundation.[25] In 1994, the William H. Donner Foundation gave $50,000 to focus *Media-Nomics* on media treatment of free enterprise and direct it to

journalists and TV executives.[26] In 1995, the Olin Foundation gave $50,000 to the Institute and the Dodge Jones Foun-
dation gave $10,000 "toward programs to restore balance in
the media."[27] Balance that year meant singling out for criticism any journalist who dared to mention that Republicans
were trying to cut Medicare (see chapter 5).

The January 1999 issue of *MediaNomics* provides a good
example of its brand of press criticism. Highlighting a December 29, 1998, *Nightline* program that examined why people
were wealthier than ever but saved virtually nothing, *Media-
Nomics* criticized the show because, as the newsletter put it,
"No one during the entire half hour spoke about the effect
high taxes have on personal savings. With the federal government garnering an increasing amount of revenues and running
a surplus, would it be prudent to cut taxes to bolster savings?
It didn't occur to anyone at *Nightline* to ask."[28]

Bozell says he works with reporters, feeding them story
ideas and making suggestions about who they should interview and how they should shape their reports. He also calls
editors and TV producers to offer his thoughts. During the
health-care reform debate, Bozell sent a letter to NBC and
talked to the executive producer complaining that the network was using Bob Dole instead of Phil Gramm to counter
the Clinton health plan. "Phil Gramm would have been a
better spokesman," Tim Graham explained. "We wanted
some sense of opposition to the Clinton health-care plan."[29]
Apparently Dole did not express enough of the outrage the
Center was looking for.

The Media Research Center also cites journalists whose
work it likes and those whose work it doesn't. Inevitably, the
constant critiques grind journalists down, and they begin to

subtly and not-so-subtly embrace the conservative spin. The organization helps create a climate to neutralize the efforts at honest reporting.

The October 1998 issue of *MediaNomics* rebuked reporters from the *Washington Post* and the *Los Angeles Times* for not discussing, in their stories about patient-protection legislation, the right wing and insurance industry positions that such laws result in cost increases that boost the number of uninsured. *MediaNomics* praised Robert Pear of the *New York Times* for mentioning opposition to the so-called health mandates in his report, although it was not cited high enough in the story to suit *MediaNomics*. The newsletter noted that Pear said in his story: "A coalition of HMOs, insurance companies and employers—the Health Benefits Coalition—vehemently opposed new federal mandates on health plans, saying such requirements would increase costs and reduce the number of people with coverage," but took him to task because "he didn't mention this argument until the eighteenth paragraph of his article."[30] The next time Pear writes a story on the subject, will he mention the cost argument higher in his story? Will other reporters include it? And what of the other costs— the human costs of not providing care, which the legislation was aiming to address? Will that be discussed, or will reporters (and editors) avoid the subject?

Likewise, the constant praise from right-wing media operations reinforces reporting that already carries the right's twist on the issues. When journalists and their work are noted favorably in the "Kudos" section of *MediaNomics,* it helps further the kind of reporting the right prefers. In December 1998, the newsletter praised *ABC World News Tonight* for being "one of the pioneers in network investigation of government waste," and pointed out that "its regular segment 'Your Money' delves into ways that Americans are being ripped off."[31] In the next issue, it lauded NBC's "Fleecing of America," a similar show that identifies ways that the government wastes taxpayers' money. *MediaNomics* called "Fleecing of America" along with "Your Money" "one of the best news segments on network television."[32] Both programs reinforce the view that government is evil, bungling, and wasteful, which is precisely the message the right wants to convey.

The Media Shift to the Right

It is impossible to quantify the influence Bozell and his colleagues have had on how the media report the issues. But there are unmistakable signs that the media have moved to the right—from the selection of panelists on the Sunday morning interview shows to the army of conservative columnists to the hiring practices at *Time*. Says Dan Goodgame, *Time's* Washington bureau chief: "We're interested in what's new and fresh and interesting and a helluva lot of what's new and fresh and interesting is conservative ideas. We've got to have people who are not just open to that but fascinated by that—eager to report on it." Goodgame says *Time* has rejected journalists with impressive writing skills because they "seemed sure that there were government programmatic solutions to problems and that what the Republicans were talking about wasn't worthy of consideration."[33]

Even the *Washington Post,* arguably the most liberal large paper in the country, doesn't always take progressive positions.

In 1995, the *Post* ran an editorial supporting Republicans

for being "gutsy" and "inventive" in proposing Medicare reforms and calling Democrats "irresponsible." The Republican National Committee turned the editorial into a television ad, prompting Kate O'Beirne, now the Washington editor of the *National Review*, to remark: "Liberals can be made to feel uncomfortable if the *Washington Post* has taken a different line from them. I'm glad now that during the Reagan years, I never canceled my subscription."[34]

Donald Graham, the *Post*'s publisher, told the late Joseph Rauh, the longtime civil rights activist, "You have to remember one thing: this is not the liberal paper that you remember." The *Post* had turned down Rauh's op-ed protesting the *Post*'s endorsement of Edwin Meese for attorney general in the Reagan administration.[35]

Public television, where one would expect to see more diverse views presented, has turned rightward as well, no doubt in response to continuous bombardment by the right-wing media monitors. In 1992, the Center for Media and Public Affairs, which has received funds from the Bradley, Olin, Smith Richardson, and Scaife foundations, published a report critiquing the programming on PBS. The study, "Balance and Diversity in PBS Documentaries," written by Robert and Linda Lichter and Daniel Amundson, concluded, "There can be little doubt that the ideas expressed on public affairs issues were far more consonant with the beliefs and preferences of contemporary American liberals than with those of conservatives."[36] Later, two sociologists from Vassar College and Virginia Commonwealth University dissected the Lichter study in "By Invitation Only: How the Media Limit Political Debate." They found shoddy research and a misleading critique. The sociologists noted that the Lichter study examined only a "tiny slice of PBS programs . . . systematically excluding the bulk of programs broadcast by PBS stations." The Lichter study, for example, looked at PBS public affairs programming by sampling only one station, WETA in Washington, D.C.[37] (The sociologists' own study revealed considerable variability in public affairs programming broadcast by other PBS stations.) They also noted that the discussion of balance in the Lichter study was based on a small percentage of documentary programming and concluded that the study ignored "the vast majority of what PBS stations air."[38]

In 1995, the Center for the Study of Popular Culture weighed in with its own report, "Public Broadcasting and the Public Trust." The authors argued that the political bias in public broadcasting has compromised its claims to disinterested public service and that broadcasters in the system have not held themselves accountable to the public. It cited PBS's sympathetic coverage of the Black Panthers in programs like "Eyes on the Prize II" and "Black Power, Black Panthers," and its coverage of the 1992 presidential election as examples of bias.[39]

Such studies have given cover to conservative members of Congress and other critics, who have used them to attack PBS. David Horowitz, who heads the Center for the Study of Popular Culture, boasted, "Probably Senator Dole and I are the two individuals that had the most to do with the present hold [on reauthorization of PBS funding]."[40] About the time the Lichters released their study, Congress held hearings on PBS funding that eventually resulted in the Public Telecommunications Act of 1992. That law directs PBS to annually review its programming to ensure "objectivity and balance in all programs or series of programs of a controversial nature."[41]

In 1995, Congressional Republicans carried the attack further, threatening to eliminate the $300 million annual subsidy for public broadcasting.[42] PBS kept its subsidy, but battle scars remained.

In the years following the 1992 act, PBS appears to have taken its new legislative mandate seriously. As critics James Ledbetter, William Hoynes, and David Croteau have documented in depth, PBS—contrary to its politically correct, liberal image—has shifted dramatically to the right. Perhaps most visible is the increasing presence of extended on-air sponsorship of programs by major multinational companies and creeping commercialization. But quite beyond that, it has changed the ideological makeup of its board of journalist advisers, has shifted the balance of its on-air guest experts toward conservative commentators—often without clearly identifying their ideologically activist affiliations—and it has watered down such signature programs as the *MacNeil/Lehrer NewsHour*. Once that program could be counted on to ask both deep and sharp questions of its guests, but it now has turned into a "he said, she said" debate, which often takes an adversarial position against the federal government. Typical probing questions are now "What's your response to that?" or "What do you think about this?"

Erwin Knoll, the longtime editor of *The Progressive* and a member of the *MacNeil/Lehrer NewsHour* panel of regional commentators, died in November of 1994. Knoll left a void that was quickly filled by the conservative Patrick McGuigan, editorial-page editor of the *Daily Oklahoman*. Without Knoll, there was no strong liberal voice on the show.

In 1997, PBS aired a segment of media criticism on a new show called *Media Matters* that claimed the press had gone astray when it reported on the plight of soldiers who had served in the Gulf War. Guests all made the same point: the media reported suspicions about the Pentagon; reporters had relied too heavily on the veterans' stories; the media should have stressed the medical and scientific evidence, which according to the show was irrefutable—chemical weapons had played no part in Gulf War illness.[43]

Two of the guests were right-wing spokesmen whose credentials were not revealed. Terry Eastland was identified as a "reporter" and "of *Forbes.*" At the time of the show, Eastland worked for Forbes Digital Media and was a senior fellow at the conservative Ethics and Public Policy Center. Michael Fumento was once a Warren T. Brookes Fellow in environmental journalism at the Competitive Enterprise Institute. When the show aired, he was a visiting scholar at the American Enterprise Institute. Fumento, who wrote in a 1995 piece for the *American Spectator* that "the closest Gulf War Syndrome comes to having a prime cause may be the American media," was identified only as a "media critic."[44] The show's executive producer, Alex Jones, admitted that Fumento was not really a media critic, but had a "perspective on the things we were looking for."[45]

Fumento's perspective, it turned out, was the only one that emerged. The appearance by Fumento, Eastland, and reporters who have sometimes agreed with the Pentagon on this issue presented a one-sided view. Two days after the PBS story aired, the *New York Times* ran a story about a new GAO report that found "substantial evidence" linking nerve gas and other chemical weapons to health problems veterans had experienced. The PBS show, however, gave no hint of the impending report that contained information contrary to the thrust of the program. Omitting a discussion of the report either made PBS look foolish or was a deliberate attempt to stack the deck.[46]

In late summer, at least half the members of a White House panel, which had once determined that stress was a major cause of Gulf War Syndrome, had reversed themselves and were about to say that chemical weapons might have played a part after all.[47] In mid-fall, the panel released its final report, saying that the Pentagon had dismissed credible evidence that thousands of marines may have been exposed to poison gas when they crossed Iraqi minefields.[48] Did PBS producers fail to do their homework, or did the new information not fit the message the program wanted to convey?

A few months before the *Media Matters* segment aired, FDA Commissioner David Kessler, who was about to leave his post, appeared on the *NewsHour with Jim Lehrer*. Margaret Warner, the show's correspondent, challenged Kessler: "Why do we need, in your view, such an activist government in protecting public health and safety? I mean fifty years ago the FDA, while it existed, was certainly not half as aggressive as it is now. And yet people didn't die by the thousands from tainted meat and drugs. Why do you feel we need such an activist agency such as yours?"[49]

By today's standards, Warner's question might seem like a provocative interviewing technique, but it also represents a major shift in journalistic mind-set. Warner tried to make Kessler justify what his agency was doing, and the question struck at the very heart of the FDA's existence. Twenty years ago, journalists mindful of the public interest would have asked why the FDA was too cozy with industry, and why it wasn't doing more to protect the public. Warner's question,

33

however, implied that the agency had gone too far in protecting the public and perhaps was no longer necessary. That was the premise of the right-wing think-tank coalition that attacked the FDA.

Repetition Is Key

Perhaps the single strategy that has made the right-wing think tanks so effective has been constant repetition of their messages in different media to different audiences. Observes one Washington journalist who declined to be identified: "Groups on the right know their purpose is to take information into the policy debate. Groups on the left think the issue is their purpose. The left thinks ten people can achieve something working by themselves. The right understands it's more effective to take ten people to convince 10,000 people to work for change. It's the leverage of propaganda."

The mere appearance of a story is not enough to affect policy, says FAIR's Jim Naureckas. "It needs to be repeated over and over for a long period of time."[50] One story does not have a lasting impression on people's political consciousness. But if the public hears the same message multiple times, soon people will believe its veracity. The public has heard so often that Medicare is bankrupt and that Social Security won't be around in thirty years, many have come to believe it, paving the way for their acceptance of the right's prescriptions for change.

Conservative organizations identified repetition in the media as a key media strategy faster than other groups, and exploited it more rigorously and energetically. Some commentators have called this the "echo" or "multiplier" effect. With generous funding from foundations, right-wing organizations have been able to take full advantage of the technique of repetition and the impact it has on public discourse. These groups have also recognized and exploited cross-class dissemination routes, appropriating the basic strategies of large commercial marketers, which advertise in a variety of media. The big, for-profit companies have learned to saturate their markets with their messages, and so have right-wing think tanks.

Right-wing groups—motivated by their strong commitment to free-enterprise ideology and well endowed with foundation money—repeat and recycle their messages, ideas, and solutions. Cato, for example, recycled its privatization message in many ways. It published a sophisticated, technical book in hardcover called *A New Deal for Social Security* for opinion leaders. At the same time, it released a simplified, less jargon-filled version for ordinary Joes: *Common Cents Common Dreams: A Layman's Guide to Social Security Privatization* is a fifty-page, pocket-size paperback complete with cartoons that promotes privatization in the most straightforward of terms.

Tidbits and snippets of information found in think-tank newsletters and press releases are recycled on radio talk shows by conservative hosts. The newsletter of the Competitive Enterprise Institute contains "endnotes" eminently suitable for the talk-show circuit. The September 1998 issue of the newsletter *CEI Update* noted that twenty years ago in Texas, three counties took advantage of a temporary legal provision that let them opt out of the Social Security system. County employees could enroll in an alternative retirement plan that paid higher returns. For some employees, the newsletter said, "the increase is greater than 20 percent." The "soundbite" concluded "No one else can take advantage of similar programs, as the opt-out provision has since been repealed."[51] Radio talk-show hosts could easily pick up that item and repeat the essential theme: People will do better if their funds are not part of the current Social Security system.

Striking Back

Foundation money for general operating support makes it easier for right-wing groups to strike back quickly when another viewpoint is expressed, tending to neutralize or even discredit the opposing opinion.

Nearly every day during November and December of 1998 and throughout 1999, the Cato Institute sent journalists a one-page fax commenting on some aspect of the effort to privatize Social Security.

Whenever a group or person produced a new study or comments refuting or questioning Cato's position, the think tank was ready to respond—sending messages to journalists even when Social Security was not high on the congressional "to do" list, always keeping the issue in front of them.

With single-mindedness, tenacity, and a $13 million budget, Cato has moved privatization from nowhere four years ago to the top of the national agenda today. "We're treating this as a full-court press until we get the job done," said Michael Tanner, Cato's director of health and welfare studies. "We have no higher priority. We won't rest or call off our project until people have control over one hundred percent of their money."[52]

The right wing's media network also stands ready to answer any opposition, with the *Washington Times,* the *Wall*

Street Journal, and other conservative publications opening their pages to right-wing analysts and academics who want to counter a position or paper that may potentially get media attention or perhaps has already gotten some.

The Cloak of Nonpartisanship

Right-wing groups have cast themselves as neutral observers more akin to professors in academic institutions that "educate" rather than to organizations that "lobby." Indeed they believe—and many in the media accept—that they have supplanted the universities as idea generators, and have assumed the public role universities once played. "Universities became less relevant to the public debate in the seventies," observed Larry Mone of the Manhattan Institute.[53]

The cloak of the academy and the nonpartisan label help disguise the agendas of right-wing groups, as well as their benefactors. This makes it easier to get the attention of editors and writers who may be more likely to use material from an "objective third party." The trappings of academe lend credibility to their work. Such trappings connote stature, impartiality, and scientific rigor, and they convey a sense of knowledge rather than ideology that makes it easier for the media to embrace their ideas. Think-tank rosters are replete with visiting scholars, senior scholars, junior scholars, visiting fellows, adjunct scholars, research fellows, senior fellows, and distinguished fellows that further the notion of objectivity, scholarly research, and impartiality. The 1997 annual report of the Cato Institute lists ten different designations for its fellows, including a "Fellow in Fiscal Policy Studies" and a "Distinguished Senior Fellow in Foreign Policy Studies."[54]

Liberal think tanks use some of the same trappings, of course. But for the most part, they embrace the academy not to influence government programs but to produce a neutral scientific evaluation of a particular activity. Conservative groups have the opposite goal. "They have a huge juggernaut of private foundation money organized by the right-wing economic elite and they pour money into these so-called think tanks to pretend that independent research verifies their world view," says Rep. David Obey, a Wisconsin Democrat who serves on the House Appropriations Committee.[55]

The IRS classifies think tanks, regardless of their ideological perspective, as 501(c)3 organizations, which means they cannot lobby in the conventional sense; they don't hire lobbyists to work Capitol Hill, and they don't give PAC money to candidates. Their tax exemption allows them to collect contributions and educate. These organizations are nonpartisan in the sense that they don't support positions of either Democrats or Republicans, take money from the government, or officially endorse legislation. But being nonpartisan doesn't mean they don't advocate their positions or encourage legislators to adopt their solutions. "We don't endorse legislation, but it's obvious reading our papers which is the best idea," says Heritage's Dan Mitchell. "Our usual role is to take things that are not well understood and put them in an understandable form for policymakers."[56]

Heritage "Backgrounder" papers carry a disclaimer that nothing in them "is to be construed as necessarily reflecting the views of The Heritage Foundation or as an attempt to aid or hinder the passage of any bill before Congress."

But sometimes the lines between education and lobbying blur. In April 1994, Heritage issued a "Backgrounder Update"

38

called "The State and District Impact of the Clinton Tax Increase." The backgrounder singled out, by Congressional district, members of Congress who had voted for the Clinton tax package in 1993. The paper, strategically timed to coincide with the April 15 tax deadline, noted that the "tax burden in America is at an all-time high" due in part to Clinton's tax increase, which Heritage said was the "largest tax increase in world history,"[57] a false assertion that made the rounds in the media. Clinton's tax law wasn't even close to the largest increase in U.S. history. The 1993 tax act raised overall taxes by about three percent. During World War II, tax increases to help pay for the war were twenty-four times as large as the Clinton increase. The surtax enacted at the end of the Johnson administration to help finance the Vietnam War was three and a half times larger, and two tax bills enacted in 1983 and 1984 to rescue Social Security and reduce the deficit raised more revenue than Clinton's 1993 tax law.[58] However, the Clinton tax reforms did reclaim some 40 percent of the remaining Reagan-era tax cuts enjoyed by the wealthiest one percent of America's families. In addition, the most well-off seniors had to pay taxes on a higher portion of their Social Security benefits, and workers with the highest incomes found that the earnings cap on the Medicare-financing portion of their payroll taxes had been lifted.[59] To the wealthiest people, who complained the loudest, the tax increase may indeed have seemed large.

Whether it's called lobbying or educating, the ability of Heritage to get local data about the effect of tax bills into the hands of journalists has won favor among the media. Says Edwin Roberts, who runs the editorial page of the *Tampa Tribune*: "If there is a major tax-cut proposal, such as the child credit business, they will run [data] through the big computer they've got and they will figure out how much extra money goes to people who live in every Congressional district. Nobody else is doing that."[60]

Heritage vice president Stuart Butler explained: "We have the ability to translate the broad rhetoric of the conservative movement into actual legislation. We show members of Congress how they can achieve the things they promised back when they were candidates."[61]

Aftermath

Charles Lindblom observed in *The Policy Making Process* (1980) that in the late 1970s, business, under attack from Nader and the consumer movement, stepped up its electoral activities.[62] But neither Lindblom nor most other observers could have predicted the far-reaching influence of think tanks set up precisely to negate the antibusiness trends that were then surfacing. Nor could they have predicted the technological revolution and changes in media ownership that have made it possible for right-wing ideas to form such a stronghold. Lindblom could not have predicted how the media would fail to challenge the new political discourse.

For its twenty-fifth anniversary, celebrated at a gala in December 1997, The Heritage Foundation stated its landmark objectives. Among them:[63]

"• a Congress that shares Heritage's vision for America
• a reinvigorated federal system where governors, legislators, and other state and local officials share Heritage's vision for America

- a public–policy research capability that is the most responsive, credible, advanced, and respected in the world"

In a speech celebrating Heritage's accomplishments, president
Edwin Fuelner declared: "Twenty-five years ago, we listened
to harangues from Ralph Nader, Jerry 'Moonbeam' Brown,
and Jane Fonda. Today, we listen to the sweet music of old
friends like Charlton Heston and Paul Harvey, and new voices
of sanity like Rush Limbaugh and Dr. Laura. Twenty-five
years ago, a smaller government seemed an unreachable goal.
Today, it seems within our grasp."[64]

Welfare reform à la Heritage has been accomplished. Medicare and Social Security, too, may be reshaped along the lines
envisioned by Heritage and sold to the public by its propaganda machine. The consequences of the assault on so many
fundamental government programs is likely to spawn a kind of
social Darwinism, with the media looking the other way. In
an interview, Brent Bozell stated his goals for the Media Research Center. His aim, he said, was for there to be no need for
his organization. "The day this organization is not needed,
I'm a happy camper," he said. "I've done my job."[65]

Heritage and Bozell are well on their way to achieving their
goals, raising the very issues that Lippmann warned about
more than seventy years ago: the false premises that debaters
have not challenged and the neglected aspects omitted from
the argument.

2
Wounding the Enemy: The Attack on AARP

"It's very critical to the Republican revolution that they take money out of advocacy groups. That money is used against the forces of fiscal restraint."[1]
——Stephen Moore
　　　Director of Fiscal Policy Studies, The Cato Institute

"We will hunt [these liberal groups] down one by one and extinguish their funding sources."[2]
——Grover Norquist
　　　President, Americans for Tax Reform

Launching the Attack

In December 1994, the Capital Research Center—a non-profit group whose self-described mission is to track the funding sources of nonprofit organizations engaged in public interest advocacy[3]—launched a bold attack on the American Association of Retired Persons (AARP) and the National Council of Senior Citizens (NCSC). Both organizations had liberal legislative agendas, and AARP, in particular, with its 33 million members—an average of 76,000 in every congressional district—represented a major impediment to the right wing's efforts to dismantle Social Security and Medicare.

43

To the right, AARP's tax-exempt status gave it "an unfair advantage" against the large insurance companies and financial conglomerates that typically support conservative causes and sell similar goods and services.[4] AARP was also a long-standing symbolic thorn in the side of the conservative movement, a behemoth as ripe for attack and discrediting as the AFL-CIO. But most important, AARP was publicly committed to protecting two of the government programs the right was most eager to see cut down: Social Security and Medicare. In the face of increasing right-wing pressure to privatize Social Security, Horace Deets, AARP's longtime president, had declared privatization to be "an unsound panacea" and warned that the "risk of planning and investment would shift to the individual." Deets had said that "Social Security has worked well for sixty years, and there is no reason to believe that it is on the verge of bankruptcy."[5] And when medical savings accounts, a right-wing insurance solution, were proposed as a cure for Medicare's financial problems, AARP dropped its support. Deets said Republicans were going "too far too fast."[6]

But like any big, entrenched organization, AARP had become an easy target for criticism, especially given its sheer size, large staff, and somewhat unsavory beginnings as an insurance sales outfit. AARP still sells insurance as well as mutual funds, and from time to time, various magazines have reported that those products are not the best its members can buy. Less often reported is the fact that AARP also sells some very good policies, such as guaranteed-issue, community-rated Medigap insurance that members can obtain even if they are unhealthy.

AARP's business interests sometimes conflict with its advocacy mission, and the attack by Capital Research struck at the intersection of those activities. It hit at the bread and butter of AARP's very existence—its tax exemption—which allows the group to sell products and avoid paying taxes on the profits as long as those profits are related to activities that benefit its members.

The attack by Capital Research began with an article in its monthly newsletter *Organization Trends,* which called into question the activities of the AARP and the NCSC. *Organization Trends* assailed AARP for:[7]

- being the second largest nonprofit organization after the Catholic Church (the article called the AARP the "900 pound guerilla [*sic*] of nonprofitdom")
- being out of sync with its members by supporting healthcare reform and championing catastrophic medical coverage. *Organization Trends* noted that "more than 70 Congressmen wrote to AARP's Executive Director Horace Deets (salary: $286,000)" saying that the group had "lost touch with the people they ostensibly represent"
- making money from arrangements with private businesses such as Prudential and the Hartford Insurance Group
- receiving $85.9 million in federal taxpayer funds in 1993: "This represents 23.9 percent of a total $358 million it reported as income," the newsletter said
- having a "palatial" Washington office with lease payments of $27.6 million that included equipment and warehouse facilities
- paying $135 million to the IRS to settle a dispute over royalty income
- embracing a liberal agenda on everything from higher taxes to gun control, and opposing a balanced-budget amend-

ment. *Organization Trends* cited a report from the National Taxpayers Union Foundation, which said that enacting AARP's agenda would increase federal spending by as much as $1 trillion over the coming decade.

Similarly, when it came to the National Council of Senior Citizens, the sins included:[8]

• receipt of government grants
• support of Democratic candidates
• "impressive" Washington headquarters
• support of such legislation as the Family and Medical Leave Act and the Motor Voter bill
• opposition to NAFTA

Capital Research staged a classic ad hominem attack, hitting the advocates, not the issues. It strung together a list of factual details about each organization and presented them in a way that demonized both, without presenting any perspective that would have put those facts in context to help people evaluate the validity of the charges. Although Capital Research made it seem that way, it's hardly a sin to be large, to pay back taxes, or to support Democratic causes or candidates that conform to the purposes of the organization. Capital Research questioned AARP's credibility and made it appear that it was engaging in some kind of heinous wrongdoing.

Organization Trends, for instance, did not mention that the government grants came from the Labor Department and the Environmental Protection Agency as payment for services AARP had performed: the administering of community-service and environmental-training programs for seniors and

helping them fill out their tax forms. The newsletter also neglected to point out that government grants don't cover all of
AARP's costs to administer those programs.

Nor did the newsletter say whether AARP's "palatial"
headquarters and Deets' salary were reasonable by Washington standards, which they were. In fact, Deets' salary was low
compared with the heads of other organizations that lobby on
similar issues: the Health Insurance Association of America,
the Blue Cross/Blue Shield Association, and the American
Medical Association, for example.

Capital Research is headquartered in a historic townhouse
on Sixteenth Street in Washington, D.C. Some of the center's
supporters, including Washington power lobbyist Tom
Korologus, Winn Dixie Stores Inc., the Sarah Scaife Foundation, Joseph Coors, the Outdoor Power Equipment Institute,
and K. Tucker Anderson, who is also a major benefactor and
board member of the Cato Institute, contributed toward the
purchase.[9]

The attack on AARP is emblematic of one strategy used by
the right wing—undermining the legitimacy of its opponents
by questioning their funding sources and casting doubt about
their motives. It falls to Capital Research, the self-appointed
attack dog of the right, to help carry out this strategy. Indeed,
the Center's 1997 annual report spelled out its mission with a
quote from Malcolm S. Forbes, Jr.: "The Capital Research
Center is determined to use information to break a peculiar
philanthropic pattern: major corporations giving money to
groups whose agendas are the antithesis of free enterprise."[10]

To this end, Capital Research publishes an annual volume
called *Patterns in Corporate Philanthropy,* a compilation of charitable giving by some 200 of the country's largest corporations.

The publication has gotten good press. In one newsletter a few years ago, Capital Research noted that media coverage of the book had carried the right spin—"The majority of head-lines for the story echoed the sentiment 'Corporations Aid the Enemy.'"[11] Capital Research has also used unfavorable coverage to its advantage. One year the *Washington Post* phoned Monsanto, a company profiled in the book, and discovered that Capital Research was wrong about the corporation's contributions. The Center's newsletter reprinted the *Post* story, and told donors that ". . . publicity is in the eye of the beholder: a couple of pokes from the liberal bastion of the *Washington Post* is not necessarily a bad thing."[12] What constituted good reporting at the *Post* gave the Center a chance to condemn the "liberal media," another of the right's effective strategies.

The Center's mission also has a media–education component. A brochure sent to prospective donors explains that part of the Center's job is to provide "insight into the world of public-interest advocacy and financing so reporters and editors can better judge the credibility of the interest group"[13]— a credibility that is judged by an organization whose own credibility, political agenda, and cadre of invisible benefactors are obscured and go largely unscrutinized by the press.

Capital Research's annual budget of about $68,000 when it was founded in 1984[14] has increased to over $1.5 million today.[15] Most of its funding comes from a handful of conservative foundations, including the Scaife Family Foundation, the Sarah Scaife Foundation, the John M. Olin Foundation, the William H. Donner Foundation, and the Lynde and Harry Bradley Foundation. Almost all of the rest comes from corporations and individuals. In 1992, the Sarah Scaife Foundation (one of four foundations associated with right-wing financier Richard Mellon Scaife) contributed $250,000,[16] or some 30 percent of the group's revenues for the year.[17]

In 1993, Capital Research received a quarter of a million dollars from the Sarah Scaife Foundation for general operating support[18] and $25,000 from the Scaife Family Foundation to finance another of its newsletters, called *Philanthropy Culture & Society*,[19] which has commented on such topics as Bill Clinton's family values, love and marriage, the private-school voucher movement, and a biblical perspective on welfare reform.[20]

The John M. Olin Foundation gave $25,000 for a report on the politicization of charity,[21] and the Lynde and Harry Bradley Foundation gave $40,000 for an analysis of the nonprofit policy agenda.[22] In 1993, the Olin Foundation also gave the group $25,000 for publications and research on federal grants to advocacy organizations.[23] (Much of Capital Research's attack on AARP and the NCSC revolved around the federal grants they received.) The Scaife foundations have continued to give generously to the Capital Research Center. In 1994, Scaife foundations gave $300,000 for the Philanthropy, Culture and Society program, general operating support, and other projects.[24] In 1996, the Sarah Scaife Foundation gave another $300,000 for general support and for the group's capital campaign.[25] In 1995, the William H. Donner Foundation chipped in $60,000 to monitor the growing influence of nonprofit public-interest advocacy groups.[26]

The Media Run with the Story

With its attack on AARP, Capital Research could not have hoped for a more cooperative press or a more direct affirmation of its mission. "Before November (1994) we could only complain," wrote Capital Research Center president Terrence Scanlon in *Capitol Reports,* another of the Center's newsletters. "Let's hope we see some response now."[27] Scanlon, a former chairman of the Consumer Product Safety Commission under Ronald Reagan, didn't have long to wait.

The Center's handiwork first surfaced in the right-wing media with an article in the *National Review* on February 6, 1995. The *Review,* a barometer of right-wing thinking, attacked the National Council of Senior Citizens, using the same facts that first surfaced in *Organization Trends.* The *National Review* conceded that the federal money was spent on jobs programs for the elderly poor and to build and manage senior citizen housing, but the magazine then implied that the grants were used for lobbying. Though it's illegal to use government funds to lobby, the *National Review* said these grants at least "indirectly help support political activism." It offered no proof.[28]

Both the NCSC and AARP are 501(c)4 organizations, which means that they have the government's blessing to lobby. They are considered social-welfare organizations; in IRS parlance, that means they have wide latitude to lobby, unlike 501(c)3 organizations, such as Capital Research, which is a "charitable" organization that can solicit tax-exempt contributions and engage only in educational activities. Organizations with 501(c)4 designations cannot use government grants for lobbying.

Next, *Organization Trends* editor Robert Pambianco attacked both groups on National Empowerment Television, a cable network dedicated to promoting conservative interests, and on the PBS show *Technopolitics.*[29] The information in *Or-*

ganization Trends also found its way into the March issue of *Intellectual Ammunition,* a publication of the Heartland Institute, a conservative think tank in Chicago.[30] But the publication, whose audience is mostly state legislators, was small fry in the food chain of influence.

A much bigger fish soon appeared. Wyoming Senator Alan Simpson picked up the work of Capital Research and became the driving force in the effort to discredit AARP. Simpson was the perfect messenger. He had power as chair of the Senate Finance subcommittee on Social Security and Family Policy, he was free from political constraint since he was about to announce his retirement from the Senate, and he had a motive.

Simpson had long been a foe of AARP, sharply disagreeing with the group's positions on Social Security, Medicare, and funding long-term care. A wealthy rancher-turned-politician and son of a former Wyoming governor, Simpson liked to tell stories about how he had to pay out of his pocket for his own parents' care and believed everyone else should do the same. He had opposed AARP's attempts to include benefits for long-term care in the Clinton health-care plan, and resented AARP's opposition to the balanced-budget amendment.

Simpson also believed that AARP was an obstacle to reforming Medicare. The organization was likely to oppose both the cuts that Republicans needed to pay for their tax reductions and the fundamental changes their allies in the right-wing think tanks wanted that would eventually convert Medicare from a social insurance program into a private insurance scheme.

Simpson used the *Washington Times* to signal his intentions, penning an op-ed on February 16, 1995, in which he soundly chastised AARP executive director Horace Deets for saying that Medicare had already been cut by about $200 billion in recent years. Simpson charged that AARP's statement was "uttered with intent to deceive" and that "such misrepresentations on the part of special-interest groups" were "the rule rather then the exception . . ."[31] Simpson was engaging in a bit of deception himself, omitting the fact that Medicare payments to doctors and hospitals had indeed been slashed, while premiums and deductibles had increased, resulting in the cuts Deets mentioned. The truth hardly mattered; the op-ed served notice that AARP's credibility was on the line.

In late March, Simpson announced that he would hold hearings on AARP's finances. As he talked to reporters in a Capitol corridor, Simpson pumped his arms and danced a little jig. "I'm a chairman," he boasted. "I can have hearings." A few days before his announcement, Simpson had said: "People ought to know where their money comes from and what it's used for."[32]

What followed was an extraordinary onslaught of media coverage, virtually all stemming from the Capital Research Center. The Center's attack was picked up and trumpeted in publications of every size in every part of the country. As spring passed into summer, an avalanche of news stories, editorials, and opinion pieces hit the public, and almost all made the same points first raised in the Capital Research newsletter and filtered through Simpson:

- The *San Diego Union Tribune* reported that Simpson said AARP would be asked about a 1994 settlement with the IRS to pay $135 million in back taxes.[33] Nonprofit organizations must pay taxes on unrelated business activities, and

AARP had gotten in hot water with the IRS and then had agreed to pay $135 million in unrelated business income taxes and penalties dating from 1983.

- The *Albany Times Union* quoted Simpson as saying, "What I see is the bloated arrogance of some of their officers. Their executive director Horace Deets gets paid $286,000 a year and he is very, very clever."[34]

- The *Atlanta Journal-Constitution* reported that Simpson questioned whether AARP "really reflects the views of its 34 million members."[35]

- The *St. Petersburg Times* allowed Simpson to spell out his top ten gripes with AARP. Among them: AARP leases a single building in Washington, D.C., for more than $17 million per year and spends another $7.6 million on additional office space each year.[36]

- The *San Francisco Chronicle* failed to question Simpson's claim that AARP had abused its tax-exempt status by publicly backing universal health insurance and opposing the balanced-budget amendment.[37]

Most distressing, though, was the degree to which the major media took up the aggressive tone and ad hominem style of the Capital Research attack. On *This Week With David Brinkley,* for example, Sam Donaldson asked AARP president Eugene Lehrmann, "Well, if you make all that money, sir, why do you need $86 million in taxpayer money?"[38] The mendacity and condescension in that statement was extraordinary even by the usual combative standards of the program. Donaldson barely allowed Lehrmann to explain what the $86 million was used for. Furthermore, any reasonable journalist ought to have distinguished between taxpayer money the organization receives and what it spends on behalf of taxpayers.

Editorials and "perspective" pieces repeated the same "facts," further expanding the impression that AARP had done something wrong and must be stopped.

- The *Indianapolis Star* opined that Simpson's challenge to seniors' organizations could result in "political combustion" with the "critical rationale" being "that the private sector–public-sector romance is too cozy for the public good when the federal government gives money to organizations that spend a nice chunk of their income on lobbying the federal government."[39]
- A *Cincinnati Enquirer* editorial headlined, "Gorilla, Simpson Is Right to Question the World According to AARP," said, "AARP is so big it has its own zip code with 1,752 employees, including 17 lobbyists," and concluded, "No wonder AARP is the biggest lobbying gorilla on Capitol Hill."[40]
- The *Arizona Republic* called AARP, "not just a voice in the great debate. . . . It is, as the *Wall Street Journal* put it, 'Washington's 800-pound gorilla,' a powerful, fearsome organization which does well by doing good, all thanks to the hapless taxpayer."[41]
- The *Providence Journal-Bulletin* flatly stated, "There are conflicts of interest. The AARP is one of the most visible and effective political and lobbying organizations on Capitol Hill, and yet 22 percent of its revenues, or some \$86 million, is generated annually from federal grants." The paper did not say what the grants were used for, and failed to explain that no grant money was ever used or could be used for lobbying, but it then went on to infer that such organi-

zations "abuse their tax-exempt status in probable violation of the law's intent."[42]

It's not hard to see how the *Journal-Bulletin* drew its conclusions. Simpson himself had said that the arrangement creates the impression that AARP is inappropriately using federal money to lobby the government for more money.[43]

- Linda Chavez also wrote a syndicated column praising Simpson. She gave a brief recitation of AARP's finances, said AARP's lobbying was "especially outrageous," and noted that the organization threw its "weight around plenty." "Fear of the seniors lobby has largely held Congress hostage when it comes to even discussing Social Security reform, which serves the country badly since the program will bankrupt the federal government if it isn't reined in," Chavez wrote. The column identified Chavez as a director of the Center for Equal Opportunity, a Washington-based think tank. It did not mention that Chavez was a member of Capital Research Center's national advisory board.[44]
- The *Wall Street Journal* weighed in, noting that "far from being a do-gooder senior lobby, AARP is the field artillery in a liberal army dedicated to defending the welfare state."[45]

Some media organizations turned to the National Taxpayers Union Foundation to add heft and "credibility" to their stories, giving the group the undeserved status of detached, objective critic. In reality, it had been the original source for some of the material Capital Research used in its attack. Paul Hewitt, who was then the center's executive director, got soundbite treatment on *ABC World News Tonight*. "AARP is a dispenser of discounts and products," he announced. "It is a self-appointed voice for senior citizens. But above all, AARP is a media giant dedicated to the exercise of raw political power."[46] Fox News Network let Hewitt say: "Consumers beware, your political soul for the price of an airline discount."[47] In a "perspective" piece, the *Atlanta Journal-Constitution* quoted Hewitt as saying that AARP is a "disingenuous organization" that has "stolen our government," a preposterous statement that the writer of the article left unchallenged.[48]

Simpson had called Hewitt as a witness at his hearing, where he offered some rules for nonprofit organizations like AARP and his own. Nonprofits should receive no federal grants, or alternatively, if they spend more than 5 percent of their budgets on lobbying, they should not receive or administer any federal grants.[49]

The National Taxpayers Union Foundation was hardly an objective critic. In 1993, it published a report written by Paul Hewitt, "What Its Members Don't Know: How the AARP Agenda Would Bankrupt America." The Capital Research Center cited this report in its own book, *Frightening America's Elderly,* released in 1996.[50]

Few news stories recognized the Simpson hearings for what they were—a smear campaign started by right-wing think tanks, laced with innuendo and false inferences. Simpson made the real purpose of the campaign clear when he met with AARP board members and staff in June and told them: "I want you to know that the intensity of my investigation will be directly related to the intensity of your fight on Medicare."

The entire exercise was an attempt to silence the AARP on subjects of great importance to its more than 33 million members, force it to defend its financial arrangements, and keep the press focused on its allegedly illegal lobbying activities and other irrelevancies, such as its size, office building, and executive salaries. "Many people on the right wing realized that AARP was the force to contend with," said John Rother, AARP's chief lobbyist. "They realized they wouldn't get anywhere unless they dealt with us as an institution."[51]

Simpson never produced a smoking gun, although he produced plenty of smoke. "I'm not here to destroy the AARP," he said when his hearings began. "But I am here to get rid of hypocrisy and duplicity."[52] Most of the press covered the Simpson hearings as a Congressional oversight matter concerning AARP's tax status. Most did not see it as a crucial, divisive tactic furthering the strategic agenda of right-wing think tanks and their funders in the upcoming debates on Medicare and Social Security. They stopped short of expanding their investigations, and did not look at other organizations engaged in similar activities. For example, Catholic Charities had received more federal money than AARP (some $218 million a year). The National Rifle Association and the Sierra Club also receive income from product endorsements, but they weren't picked on, and the Republicans were trying to repeal the minimum corporate tax rate that applied to hundreds of for-profit corporations. That wasn't discussed much either in the context of organizations that paid insufficient taxes. If the media had ignored or played down Simpson's efforts, it's questionable whether his attack would have had such far-reaching consequences.

Many in the media missed the Medicare connection altogether, and the few that did get it cast their stories on the side of the attacker. *Newsweek* columnist Joe Klein wrote: "It [AARP] can continue its reflexive opposition to entitlement reform . . . or it can begin to recognize that its past successes, which won an unprecedented level of security for the elderly, have now imperiled the nation's financial security and that it's time to think about the future."[53]

An editorial in the *Sacramento Bee* concluded: "Deets is a bespectacled man who might be mistaken for a choir director. The unspoken warning he had received was that he had better play ball on Medicare."[54]

The media failed to ask the most basic of questions: What was the $86 million in taxpayer funds actually used for? They didn't ask who benefited from the grants administered by AARP. Anecdotes and "people" stories, the media's usual technique for drawing conclusions, were noticeably absent from the reportage. The *Los Angeles Times* was one of the few papers to investigate how the federal money was spent. The paper put a human face on the issue when it quoted a seventy-six-year-old retired chemical engineer who was sent to AARP for job training after suffering a stroke. When he recovered, the man landed a job with a nonprofit refugee-aid program. "This organization is taking the people who have been dumped by society and making them feel they're still part of the process," he told the *Times*.[55]

Nor did the press question who was behind Simpson's attack. During his hearings, Simpson accused the AARP of "hypocrisy and duplicity." But that charge more accurately describes the secret attack dogs that piqued Simpson's interest in the first place. National Public Radio commentator Matt Miller told his listeners in mid-July: "Simpson's strategy is starting to pay off. We've now seen a flurry of reports examining AARP's practices. But a troubling question lingers. Why did it take Simpson's action to get the press to cover what they know to be one of the most powerful institutions in

American politics? . . . This kind of stenography journalism is the rule."[56] Miller got it wrong. Simpson's attack succeeded largely *because* of stenography journalism.

That AARP supports the interests of the elderly and promotes programs beneficial to them is no secret that needs explaining. AARP has always been candid about its mission and financial arrangements with sellers of insurance products. It's not surprising that neither Simpson nor the press found anything wrong.

The agendas and motives of those attacking AARP were hardly so open. But the press didn't look for them with even a fraction of the energy it expended on AARP.

A Giant Silenced

AARP began to play ball. Toward the autumn of 1995, a few reporters noticed that AARP was sitting on the sidelines in the Medicare debate. That year Republicans aimed to cut Medicare by $270 billion and begin the process of getting the government out of the program. Said one reporter at the time: "You just can't get sharp comments even from groups you know oppose the hell out of these proposals. Gingrich has been incredibly effective in freezing all the players."[57] The *Hartford Courant* reported that AARP lobbyist Tricia Smith went so far as to compliment Heritage Foundation vice president Stuart Butler for paying attention to consumer protection details in the Heritage proposal for Medicare, which became the blueprint for the Republican plan.[58]

AARP exhibited soft opposition to the changes Republicans had in mind. A high official at the Health Care Financing Administration who was heavily involved in the politics of the

Republican proposals was blunt: "They sold out to Gingrich."

Rother later said that he did not agree with that "characterization." He added that AARP was not opposed to cutting Medicare or some of the other changes Republicans wanted, but it did not want the cuts to be as large. AARP's slogan became "too much too soon." "Because of our work with Clinton, we knew these proposals weren't going into law," Rother recalled. "We didn't have to go all out or go crazy."[59]

Although some in the media noted lukewarm opposition from AARP, most reporters did not dig out the reasons for AARP's silence or explore the connection between AARP and the right wing's agenda. They were searching for another scandal involving a large nonprofit organization—another United Way exposé. They did not find it.

The Simpson hearings discovered no impropriety or wrongdoing, but Simpson got Congress to pass as part of the lobbying reform act a provision that forbids organizations with 501(c)4 tax status, such as AARP, from accepting federal grants or loans. (In response, AARP uses the AARP Foundation, a subsidiary with a 501(c)3 tax status, to administer its federal job-training grants, and it continues to lobby as it has always done.)

The Capital Research Center and Simpson turned AARP into a less vociferous critic of conservative proposals to change Medicare and Social Security. In 1997, AARP was not a visible or vocal opponent of changes Republicans made to Medicare in the Balanced Budget Act. When the media mentioned AARP, it was often to question the group's credibility. The *New York Times,* for example, published an editorial in May 1996, "Can You Trust the AARP?," challenging its business interests.[60] *NBC Nightly News* featured Pennsylvania senator Rick Santorum who said, "the best description of the AARP is the ostrich. They just simply have their head buried in the sand and hope that all these problems with these seniors' programs that we're looking at will just simply go away." The Media Research Center's *MediaNomics* gave kudos to NBC correspondent David Bloom for challenging AARP. Said Bloom, "without the backing of Horace Deets' powerful lobby" any long-term reform of Medicare "may be impossible."[61]

AARP did not oppose the private fee-for-service option, one of the new choices Medicare beneficiaries have, and arguably the worst feature of the Balanced Budget Act. Instead of overtly opposing that provision, AARP's strategy was to attach consumer protections to discourage sellers from offering it.[62] Those protections are weak.

"Gingrich came to respect our position," Rother said. "He felt we were reasonable, and out of that perception he got the idea of appointing Deets to the Medicare Commission."[63] It was well known that AARP wanted a seat on the commission that had the potential for redefining Medicare for the next century. Gingrich did appoint Deets, who subsequently refused the offer because he would not agree to Gingrich's quid pro quo: that his appointees would not vote to raise taxes to improve the program and strengthen its finances.

AARP has been similarly subdued on Social Security reform. "They have been fairly responsible on this issue," says Michael Tanner, director of health and welfare studies for the Cato Institute. "They have not demagogued it."[64]

AARP doesn't have a proposal of its own, and it has taken a soft approach. "We have not demagogued it," admits

Rother. "We're open to private accounts on top of Social Security but not instead of Social Security. Our strategy is to work with both sides of the aisle."[65]

The January 1998 issue of *Organization Trends* showed just how reasonable the AARP had become. The newsletter attacked the National Council of Senior Citizens for promoting a liberal agenda and "opposing any policy ideas that do not promote big government and more federal spending on seniors." *Organization Trends* also attacked NCSC's position on Social Security privatization: "The efforts to privatize Social Security by creating personal savings accounts receive no consideration from NCSC."[66]

Unlike the issue published in December 1994 that kicked off the campaign against the AARP, the January newsletter focused only on the National Council of Senior Citizens. This time AARP was barely mentioned.

In late December of 1998, when Social Security reform jumped ahead on the agenda, the *Wall Street Journal* ran a story whose headline appeared to say it all: "AARP, Usually Vocal, Opts for a Neutral Stance in Politically Volatile Debate on Social Security."[67] Perhaps even more telling was an editorial appearing in the AARP bulletin in the summer of 1999. Deets wrote to his members that there was an "array of constructive—though divergent—proposals" before them, and urged that "Congress should press ahead with a plan to reform Social Security to ensure its long-term solvency. The sooner we act, the more options we have, and the less drastic the reform measures will be." Deets' commentary did not oppose privatization schemes or acknowledge, as many progressive organizations have, that there is little urgency to tear up Social Security at the moment.[68]

Aftermath

The right's attack on AARP and the NCSC had other repercussions. For the last few years, Congress has refused to reauthorize the Older Americans Act, which authorizes a variety of services for the elderly. Under the act, which passed in 1965, millions of people over age sixty receive home-delivered meals, meals in senior centers, transportation services, and other assistance so they can live at home and avoid costly nursing-home stays. The act also establishes job-training programs for low- and moderate-income elderly, run by several senior-citizen organizations including the National Council of Senior Citizens, Green Thumb, and the National Council on Aging, as well as AARP.

Some congressional Republicans, who want some of those organizations to disappear, have insisted on eliminating job-training programs as a condition for reauthorizing the act. With no funding, the organizations are effectively gone from the political process.

Meanwhile, other services provided under the act are in jeopardy if there is no reauthorization. Without it, programs could be folded into block grants, and services would be provided at the whim of the states. Services, already limited in many areas, could grow even scarcer. Despite consensus from many quarters that the act should be reauthorized, some members of Congress are still able to delay the bill reauthorizing the Older Americans Act. Unless the act is reauthorized, the only national framework for providing services to a growing elderly population is at risk.

3

Removing an Obstacle: "Modernizing" the FDA

"CEI's continued effort to dramatize the deadly effects of government regulation (CAFE, FDA, food safety) made possible the reframing of the policy debate, stripping away the mantle of virtue that has made reform so difficult. As this intellectual barrage cleared away some of the barriers to change, we moved from the intellectual artillery to the trench warfare situation more suited to specific regulatory reform. CEI's outreach work is intended to provide the reformist Congress the intellectual and moral cover needed to advance into hostile policy terrain, to liberate as much of the American economy as quickly as possible from the oppressive hand of the bureaucrats."
—Competitive Enterprise Institute, 1994 Annual Report[1]

On September 24, 1997, the Senate passed a bill overhauling the Food and Drug Administration. Except for a failed filibuster by Sen. Edward Kennedy, who warned that changes the Upper House was about to make would have dangerous consequences for the public, the bill sailed through. It had no trouble passing in the House, and a few weeks later, in November, President Clinton signed the FDA Modernization Act of 1997.[2]

With bipartisan support, Congress "modernized" the nation's oldest regulatory agency responsible for the safety of foods, drugs, cosmetics, and medical devices. The law was the culmination of a three-year effort by right-wing think tanks—The Heritage Foundation, the Competitive Enterprise Institute, Citizens for a Sound Economy, Cato, and the Washington Legal Foundation—to loosen regulation over the nation's pharmaceutical industry and makers of medical devices. Effectively using a mix of public-relations gimmicks, weighty analyses, and misleading advertising, the think tanks ganged up on the FDA and succeeded in getting a new law that:

- allows manufacturers of drugs and medical devices to advertise "off label" uses for their drugs—uses other than those for which the FDA has approved the product
- permits device manufacturers to select, negotiate, and pay private, for-profit firms to review their products instead of the independent FDA staff
- reduces the number of clinical investigations required to establish the safety and effectiveness of a drug or device from two or more studies to one or more
- makes tracking and post-market surveillance of very high-risk medical devices, such as heart valves, optional on the part of the agency rather than mandatory. These provisions vitiate consumer protections established in the 1980s after certain medical devices implanted in patients caused injury and death.

The Food and Drug Administration is one of the nation's oldest regulatory agencies, with roots going back to the days of the muckrakers who first exposed health and safety hazards in foods and drugs. Through the years, Congress has gradually given the FDA greater regulatory power over the nation's food supply, drug and cosmetics industry, and medical-device manufacturers. The passage of the FDA Modernization Act marked the worst assault on the agency's ability to protect consumers and patients in ninety-one years.[3]

The agency regulates more than $1 trillion worth of products annually—some twenty-five cents of every dollar spent each year by consumers. It has the power to bring legal sanctions against manufacturers by going to court to force them to stop selling a product or to have items seized and destroyed. It can also seek criminal penalties against manufacturers and distributors.[4]

Shortly after the 1994 elections, conservatives launched a bold assault on government regulation of all kinds. Antiregulation fever, was, of course, nothing new. A tension has always existed between corporate interests and the public interest when it comes to regulating health and safety. In the new Republican order, though, the opportunity arose to roll back regulations that corporations, conservative foundations, and think tanks found objectionable. It was a chance to reverse many of the rules and regulations won by consumer and environmental advocates in the 1960s and 1970s.

The FDA, no stranger to public criticism, was a perfect target. This time, however, the attack on the agency was different; it was not an isolated, aggrieved business or a single consumer group blasting the agency for regulating too much or too little. Think tanks orchestrating the assault had significant financial backing and determination to discredit the agency and to plant doubt about the FDA in the public's mind. Some $34 million in campaign contributions from pharmaceutical companies and medical-device manufacturers also helped soften up Congress.[5]

The right-wing attack on the FDA was in some ways a long-delayed reaction to the Kefauver Amendments, which were added to the Food, Drug, and Cosmetics Act in 1962. Those amendments, which heralded the modern era of drug regulation, required the FDA to make sure that drugs were both safe and efficacious—a process that takes years as well as millions of dollars. After passage of the Kefauver Amendments, urgency to speed up drug approvals became a way of life at the agency. The pressure intensified in the late 1980s when organizations representing the interests of people with particular diseases, such as AIDS, wanted faster approval of drugs that could potentially help those stricken. About the same time, the Quayle Commission, set up during the Bush presidency, was examining the feasibility of privatizing governmental functions, including the FDA's oversight of pharmaceuticals.

In 1993, in response to the pressure, the agency began collecting user fees from drug companies; it expanded its staff and shortened the time it took to approve new drugs. New drug approvals increased by some 40 percent,[6] an improvement that apparently was not good enough for some segments of the drug industry. "Our major concern is getting drugs out to patients quicker," the chief lobbyist for the Pharmaceutical Research and Manufacturers Association of America told the *Orlando Sun-Sentinel* in 1995.[7]

That year an unusual confluence of interest groups— ideological think tanks, pharmaceutical companies, and disease-group activists—came together to viciously attack the FDA. The result, said Thomas Moore, a senior fellow in health policy at George Washington University Medical Center, "was a relentless, narrow debate that focused on how fast drugs can be approved and eroded the FDA's essential role that a drug should be properly tested and results independently evaluated." Most new drugs are "me too" products, ones that offer very small advances. Many of those new products are simply drugs that work in a new or different way, and it often takes years before it can be shown that a new drug is indeed a therapeutic advance that improves health. "Genuine breakthroughs are rare," says Moore. "That highly life-saving drugs are being delayed doesn't reflect reality."[8] Media hype and hoopla that surround the introduction of new drugs, most of which is fostered by pharmaceutical companies, contributes to the widespread impression that most drugs are breakthroughs and that when one is kept off the market, the public suffers.

Nevertheless, public perception that drugs were being withheld from a limited number of very sick patients provided cover for the larger interests of pharmaceutical manufacturers, which wanted new marketing opportunities; their allies in the right-wing think tanks saw an attack on the FDA as a way to further erode the government's standing to protect its citizens. Fred W. Lyons, who was the chief executive officer of Marion Merrill Dow, told *Newsday*'s Saul Friedman that the industry was targeting for repeal the 1962 amendments that required drugs to be proven effective as well as safe and that the aim of the drug industry was to strip part of the FDA's regulatory power over the short run and, if necessary, replace the agency.[9] Robert Moffit, Heritage Foundation's health analyst, told Friedman, "The FDA is an example of gross interference by government with the free market."[10]

The Intellectual Barrage Begins

The task of discrediting the FDA was not going to be easy, as Republican pollster Frank Luntz made clear in a report he circulated to Republicans in 1995. Citizens for a Sound Economy, one of the anti-FDA think tanks, had paid Luntz's polling firm, Luntz Research, $50,000 to gauge public attitudes about the agency.[11] Luntz, who had helped Republicans frame their "Contract with America," discovered that the public liked the FDA, the agency enjoyed a high approval rating, and that 90 percent of Americans were confident that drugs were safe.[12]

Luntz needed a strategy to chip away at the FDA's favorable standing among the public. In his report, Luntz argued that effective communications about the agency meant:

- stressing a "corporate partnership for safety—give producers the responsibility and latitude to decide how to make safer products"
- using "new paradigms—we can achieve a safer product by updating the process"
- talking about "better science—bureaucracies are stuck in the past—apply the latest knowledge"
- pushing "safer end results—it's not deregulation; it's a better outcome we are advocating"[13]

Luntz cautioned against using the more conventional antigovernment pitch. He told Republicans to avoid the argument about cutting waste. "Nobody cares if the FDA wastes money," he said, and warned that "unlike welfare, federalism arguments do not wash here."[14] Indeed, the legislation embodied the notion of Luntz's new paradigm—modernizing the FDA. The very names of both the House and Senate bills carried the word "modernization," a testament to the coalition's power in reframing the debate about FDA. The Senate bill was called The Food and Drug Administration Modernization and Accountability Act of 1997, and the House bill was named The Prescription Drug User Fee Reauthorization and Drug Modernization Act of 1997.

About the same time that Luntz was mapping his battle plan, *The American Spectator* fired the opening barrage with a lengthy piece by James Bovard in its January 1995 issue. The article, decidedly one-sided, accused the FDA of confiscating millions of dollars of inventory from pharmaceutical and other companies, destroying thousands of private-sector jobs, and setting "grim records with its absurd delays of the approvals for new medical devices, and strangling the free exchange of information about new and innovative uses for medicines."

Bovard cited a survey that found Minnesota firms had planned to create 1,700 jobs in foreign countries over the next five years instead of in the U.S., largely because of FDA delays in approving medical devices. He recited the "horror" story of how the FDA had used its power to raid a Washington state health clinic that was dispensing—in the FDA's view— dangerous injectable B vitamins.

Bovard also attacked the FDA for coming down hard on the nutritional supplement industry, and he argued that its proposed regulations impeded the "public's right to know which substances might make them healthier and stronger." Bovard noted that the FDA staff assigned to regulating the vitamin and nutritional supplement industry had increased fourfold since 1992. He attacked FDA commissioner David

Kessler, calling him "Washington's most powerful bureaucratic czar," and challenged Congress: "One of the clearest test cases of whether a Republican Congress can begin to rein in big government will be the forthcoming battle over the future of the FDA."[15]

About the time *The American Spectator* appeared on the newsstands, Bovard wrote a commentary piece for the *Washington Times* in which he attacked Kessler's "passion for suppressing information about off-label uses of drugs" and charged that the FDA "could actually increase its repression of American drug companies." Both articles identified Bovard as the author of *Lost Rights: The Destruction of American Liberty.*[16] They did not identify his other affiliations. At the time, he was an associate policy analyst at the Cato Institute and an adjunct analyst at the Competitive Enterprise Institute, whose work he cited in his stories.[17] Cato and CEI both figured prominently in the campaign to weaken the FDA.

Bovard's criticisms began to circulate almost immediately in the conservative press. In her syndicated column, Mona Charen attacked the FDA, citing Bovard's *American Spectator* story and repeating some of the examples of agency overreach that Bovard had used.[18] Heritage Foundation president Edwin Fuelner contributed a January 10, 1995, op-ed in the *Washington Times* in which he argued that "as government grows, our freedoms shrink." He cited the FDA's "police powers which it uses to conduct secret raids on unsuspecting businesses while its real mission—protecting the public health—is held hostage to an outdated bureaucratic concept of risk that keeps life-saving technologies off the market."[19]

In 1995, The Heritage Foundation published a book called *Red Tape in America: Stories From the Front Line,* a collection of horror stories about the evils of government regulation. Among them was the tale of the FDA's raid on the Washington state health clinic that dispensed the questionable Vitamin B complex—the same example used by Bovard that was making its rounds in the media.[20]

The attack by Heritage was not a disinterested and objective evaluation of government policy, but one that couldn't help but benefit one of its largest supporters, the Amway Corporation, a privately held company based in Ada, Michigan. The company's Nutrilite division is one of the world's largest manufacturers of branded vitamins and minerals in tablet and capsule form, with some thirty different products, including herbal supplements and weight-loss pills.[21] Amway and the Van Andel Foundation are listed as Heritage "Founders" who contribute $100,000.[22] Jay Van Andel was one of Amway's founders, and his son is currently the company's chairman. According to Heritage's 1997 annual report, Amway gave Heritage $500,000, and the Jay and Betty Van Andel Foundation pledged $5 million to support domestic policy studies and programs.[23]

The assault on the FDA came right after Amway and other firms marketing dietary supplements tangled with the agency over the regulation of their products, notably the documentation needed by dietary-supplement firms to substantiate the assertions of health benefits for their products. The FDA held considerable power over Amway's Nutrilite line, which includes its Double X/TripleX multivitamin-multimineral supplement. During 1993 and 1994, Amway and its allies waged a well-funded lobbying campaign to persuade Congress to get the FDA off their backs; Amway alone channeled some $2.5 million in soft money to Republicans,[24] giving the company the distinction of being the largest soft-money donor for that election cycle. The company also donated some $306,000 in campaign contributions to candidates and the political parties, and contributions from its employees and distributors made it the sixth largest donor on the list of top individual contributors compiled by the Center for Responsive Politics.[25]

In 1994, Amway and other health-food sellers persuaded Congress to curb the FDA's regulatory power over the labeling of nutritional supplements. Congress also stripped the agency of its power to subject nutritional supplements to pre-market safety evaluations that are required of other new food ingredients or for new uses of old food ingredients. After the law was changed, nutritional supplement makers did not need FDA approval before making nutritional claims for their products.[26] Before, they did.

Dr. William B. Schultz, the FDA's deputy commissioner for policy, told the *New York Times* in the fall of 1998 that, prior to the change in the law, if the agency had concerns about a supplement it could order the substance off the market until the manufacturer proved it safe. "The biggest impact was that a lot of products probably never got to market," Schultz said. After 1994, the FDA had to prove a product is unsafe before ordering it off the market. In practice, that meant that a hazardous product could go undetected until someone is hurt. Indeed, that was the case for several dietary supplements. The *New England Journal of Medicine* reported in the fall of 1998 that a dozen people had been harmed. The *Journal's* executive editor noted: "I think this is the tip of the iceberg."[27]

In the meantime, Amway's sales had boomed, reaching a record $7 billion in fiscal 1997. In 1992, they were about $4 billion.[28] A company spokesperson says its Nutrilite division sold about $1.1 billion worth of products in fiscal 1998—not a bad return for the company's contributions to members of Congress and The Heritage Foundation.

Other Groups Weigh In

The efforts of The Heritage Foundation and *The American Spectator* were just the openers. Other groups pursued strategies of their own. Newt Gingrich's Progress & Freedom Foundation collected some $400,000 from drug, biotechnology, and medical-device companies to hire consultants, who drafted a proposal for replacing the FDA and transferring its oversight functions to private companies.[29]

Citizens for a Sound Economy sent its chairman, C. Boyden Gray, to testify in Congress against the agency. Gray, a one-time White House counsel and head of George Bush's deregulation team, is now a Washington lawyer with the firm of Wilmer, Cutler, and Pickering. In his testimony, Gray cited the same examples noted in the Bovard article and in Heritage's *Red Tape in America*. Gray also told Congress that 80 percent of those questioned (in CSE's poll by Frank Luntz) thought that if a drug has been approved and safety is not in question, the government should not restrict information about alternative benefits for which the drug was not originally approved.[30]

About the same time, CSE issued the results of Luntz's poll, spending some $60,000 for ads on Washington radio stations, publicizing the poll's results and the need for FDA reform.[31] The *BNA Health Care Daily* picked up the release and reported that the "vast majority" of Americans believe the agency is inefficient; its lengthy approval process results in lost lives and higher medical costs; and 65 percent of respondents said the agency's approval procedures discourage the invention of new medical products in the U.S.[32] CSE's press release left out a crucial finding, however, the same one Frank Luntz noted in his memo to Republicans: that the public gives the agency a high approval rating, some 72 percent of whom said that drugs and foods are safer in the U.S. Saul Friedman in a story for *Newsday* noted the omission.[33]

The Washington Legal Foundation, one of the right wing's legal arms, has received funds from foundations for specific FDA activities. In 1994, the Olin Foundation gave $150,000 for litigation on regulatory practices of the FDA, and the Samuel Roberts Noble Foundation contributed $20,000 for a program on FDA off-label drug information.[34] In 1995, the M. J. Murdock Charitable Trust contributed $200,000 for a free-enterprise communications program.[35] The Carthage Foundation, associated with Richard Mellon Scaife, has also given generously. In 1993, Carthage gave more than $1 million to the Washington Legal Foundation, and it gave another $350,000 in 1994.[36] It also got a three-year grant of $150,000 in 1992 from the Lilly Endowment, whose funds come from stock in Eli Lilly & Co., a major pharmaceutical firm.[37] The group spent about $100,000 placing more than twenty ads in influential publications such as the *New York Times, National Journal,* the *Washington Post*, and the *Washington Times*. The ads attacked the FDA.[38] One carried the headline "If a Murderer Kills You, It's Homicide—If a Drunk Driver Kills You, It's Manslaughter—If the FDA Kills You, It's Just Being Cautious." The ad listed several examples of the FDA's "over-caution":[39]

- the FDA's withholding approval for the Sensor Pad, a device used to detect breast lumps. The ad said that in Canada the product was approved in less than sixty days, and noted that the *Wall Street Journal* and ABC's *20/20* had been critical of the FDA's stubbornness.
- the FDA's delayed approval of the blood-clotting drug TPA, which the ad claimed may have saved more than 150,000 heart-attack victims
- the FDA's tardy approval of tacrine, a drug for the treatment of Alzheimer's disease. The ad said thousands of patients gradually lost their memories, and "nobody knows how many died."
- the FDA's delay in approving the cardio-pump, which the ad claimed could have saved 14,000 heart-attack victims over the two years "the FDA has delayed approval."
- an estimate made by the American Heart Association that at least 1,000 lives were lost during the time an approved heart defibrillator was delayed.

The ads were misleading and deceptive. For each claim, there was an untold story that pointed up the holes in the Washington Legal Foundation's claims.

The claim that Canada had approved the pad in sixty days was false. It had *never* been approved there, and Canadian officials ordered it off the market when the manufacturer failed to supply the same information the FDA had requested.[40] The FDA had delayed approval of the Sensor Pad because the manufacturer had not provided sufficient data to prove that the pad was effective in detecting breast lumps.[41] One promotor of the erroneous information was ABC's *20/20* correspondent John Stossel, whose work often carries a conservative twist. In his report on FDA in the summer of 1994, Stossel stated, "In Canada, they approved this [the Sensor Pad] in less than sixty days."[42] The inaccuracy rolled into the public domain and right into the hands of Citizens for a Sound Economy.

The Luntz poll that CSE had commissioned asked a question based on the erroneous information. The question stated: "The 'Sensor Pad' is a device designed to help women detect breast cancer. It was approved in Canada within sixty days. The FDA estimates that it will take nine years of testing for approval. Do you favor or oppose the fact that it will take nine years of testing for approval?" Seventy-seven percent were opposed, and 18 percent favored the approval process— hardly a surprising result given the biased question. FDA officials said that the agency had never told the company that approval would take nine years.[43]

As for the drug TPA, it also turns out that no one was at risk while the FDA was reviewing its safety and efficacy, contrary to what the Washington Legal Foundation had claimed in its ad. Another equally effective drug, streptokinase, was on the market, and doctors and hospitals were free to use it.[44] But that hardly benefited Genentech Inc., which stood to gain from a quick FDA decision on TPA. The drugmaker was poised to market TPA as the branded drug Activase for eight times the price of streptokinase.[45]

As for tacrine, there was no evidence that the drug prevented deaths from Alzheimer's disease or delayed its progression. Early studies on the drug were badly flawed and produced liver toxicity in a significant proportion of patients, so the FDA had asked for more trials. The agency also said there is no evidence that the drug prevents patients from dying from Alzheimer's or prevents progression of the mental deterioration caused by the disease.[46]

Studies on the cardio-pump showed no significant benefits over traditional CPR; even one of the study investigators conceded that the device needed more study.[47]

When it came to the defibrillator, the American Heart Association called the Washington Legal Foundation ad "irresponsible" and "incorrect," and denied making the claim about the defibrillator that the ad had attributed to the group.[48]

Incensed over the false and deceptive advertising, the FDA wrote to Washington Legal Foundation chairman Daniel Popeo noting "a number of factual errors and misleading representations about the Food and Drug Administration" and admonished Popeo to be "more accurate and factual" in future advertising.[49]

Accurate or not, the ads sparked press attention. Media outlets covered the Washington Legal Foundation's attack. Most reporters built their stories around the premise of conservative critics. The Associated Press carried a story on its wires that led with a description of one of the Washington Legal Foundation's ads. The story then noted how conservative critics are trying to persuade Congress "to dramatically restructure—or even dismantle" the Food and Drug Administration, and presented a quote from Brent Bahler of Citizens for a Sound Economy: "This is going to be a serious effort. The FDA may be doing more harm than good."[50]

The *Washington Post* and *Consumer Reports* questioned the truthfulness of some of those claims, but most of the media did not.[51] The *New York Times* ran a comprehensive story on February 12, 1995. It discussed the conservative attack, strung together quotes from pharmaceutical-industry sources who said they really didn't want to destroy the FDA, and cited a study from the Ralph Nader–affiliated Health Research Group showing that other countries had allowed more hazardous drugs on the market. It listed the amounts of some political contributions made by conservative foundations and showed a picture of one of the Washington Legal Foundation ads. But the *Times* did not touch the veracity of the advertising claims made by the Washington Legal Foundation.[52]

In an interview with the trade publication *Medical Marketing & Media,* Popeo complained that the *Times* article was an example of "pro-FDA prejudice in the media." Popeo objected to the link the *Times* had made between his organization and the anti-FDA coalition and its conservative funding sources. Nevertheless, he conceded that having his ad mentioned in a prominent news story in the *Times* was a good thing. As he saw it, the "message obtained additional exposure."[53] That was the point. By failing to challenge the claims made in the ads, the *Times* gave credibility to the Washington Legal Foundation and unintentionally helped spread its message.

A New Message: Deadly Overcaution

The Competitive Enterprise Institute, one of the most visible groups in the coalition, used the media in other ways. Founded in 1984, CEI is an offshoot of the American Enterprise Institute. With an annual budget of about $3 million,[54] it had received money from such corporations as Pfizer, Philip Morris, Coca-Cola, and Texaco, and such foundations as the Chrysler Corporation Fund, the Eli Lilly Foundation, and the Ford Motor Company Fund, as well as the Bradley, Lambe,

Starr, Sarah Scaife, and Scaife Family foundations. With a $40,000 grant, the Bradley Foundation has helped fund its "death by regulation" project[55] to promote the notion that more regulation can harm the quality of life.

Under Fred Smith, an ex–policy analyst at the Environmental Protection Agency, CEI wants to liberate the American economy from regulation[56]; many of its programs are aimed at killing regulations of one sort or another, including those affecting the automobile industry.

CEI's role in the attack on the FDA began with a press conference in mid-January of 1995 to announce its "modest proposal" for gutting the agency's regulatory authority by eliminating its approval power over drugs and devices and allowing private agencies to certify their safety and effectiveness. Under CEI's plan, drugs and devices that did not meet the agency's standards would still be available to the public, but with warning labels that disclosed the products had not received the FDA's approval.

CEI coined the slogan "deadly overcaution" and successfully promoted the notion of "drug lag." It cleverly reframed the idea of "victims," borrowing a page from Nader's book. Before 1995, said general counsel Sam Kazman, CEI had lots of ideas, but "they weren't making much impact." One way to change all that, he explained, was to take ideas out of monographs and put them into play—in other words, to look at new kinds of victims. CEI turned the idea of government regulation on its head and began to speak of "deadly regulation." The FDA "whose middle name was safety ended up killing people," Kazman said.[57]

CEI's press conference generated some "respectable" press interest, Kazman said, including an editorial in the *Chicago*

Tribune that promoted CEI's message of "deadly over-caution."[58] The editorial also supported the aims of the nutritional-supplement manufacturers, saying that vitamin makers should be given "more latitude to publicize scientific evidence that a particular vitamin or mineral may reduce one health risk or another."[59]

About the same time, CEI ran a series of radio and television public-service ads to warn people of FDA's lag in approving new drugs. The essential message: If the government approves a drug that will start saving lives tomorrow, then how many people died yesterday waiting for the government to act?

CEI had hoped the ads would be as effective in wounding the FDA as the health insurance industry's "Harry and Louise" ads had been in crippling health-care reform a few years earlier. CEI hoped that the ads would be picked up as news items like the Harry and Louise ads had been. However, Kazman said, they were not. Nonetheless, some news organizations — including CNN, *CBS Morning News,* and *NBC Nightly News*—found them sufficiently titillating to mention.[60]

Throughout 1995, the Competitive Enterprise Institute hammered away at its thesis of regulatory evil. In May, it opened a new front. It petitioned the Bureau of Alcohol, Tobacco and Firearms (BATF) to allow alcoholic-beverage labels to carry statements discussing the health benefits of moderate alcohol consumption, something BATF regulations prevented. CEI cited studies showing that the benefits of moderate consumption reduced the risk of heart attacks.[61]

Its "Vino Veritas" or free-speech wine campaign was launched not so much out of concern for the cardiovascular well-being of overweight Americans but as an oblique way of attacking the FDA's position on advertising off-label uses for drugs. Even though the press release claimed the "BATF is preventing consumers from receiving truthful, useful information," CEI had another goal in mind. As Kazman explained, "We think for the BATF to change its policy may be an inroad into the whole FDA policy."[62] In other words, if CEI could get the agency to change its position on alcoholic-beverage labeling, the FDA might be forced to allow off-label advertising for pharmaceuticals.

The media reported the story simply as another interest group petitioning a government agency. Reporters did not make the underlying connections—how relaxing the ban on alcohol advertising and the precedent it could set for advertising off-label drug uses might help some of CEI's supporters, Pfizer, for example.

Several months later, CEI commissioned a poll that found that some 58 percent of Americans knew nothing about the benefits of moderate drinking and only 10 percent were accurately informed about the benefits of moderate alcohol consumption.[63] This time virtually no stories appeared.

In early 1996, however, several publications carried a *Boston Globe* column chiding the BATF for not allowing the labeling sought by CEI and calling the Competitive Enterprise Institute one of "Washington's feistiest think tanks." The column did not delve into CEI's reasons for promoting the labeling changes.[64]

In 1997, the issue got a boost when the wine industry asked for wine labels to include statements about the benefits of moderate alcohol consumption. The BATF declined CEI's petition (several senators had threatened the agency's funding if they proceeded with the labeling change). CEI sued BATF, and the matter went to court.

In early February 1999, the Bureau of Alcohol, Tobacco and Firearms ruled that the wine industry could put labels on wine bottles encouraging consumers to learn about the benefits of drinking wine. One label approved by the BATF tells consumers to send for the Government's Dietary Guidelines and gives the address of a government agency where they can get information. Another tells consumers to ask their doctor about the health effects of wine consumption.[65]

The labels are contentious. Some public health advocates believe they will undermine efforts to raise awareness of alcohol abuse, one of the nation's biggest health problems. Michael Massing, a writer who has studied the nation's drug problems, raised these points in an op-ed in the *New York Times*. He attributed the labeling change to the clout and money of the wine industry. He didn't mention the work of the Competitive Enterprise Institute in pushing the labeling changes.[66]

Kazman says the new labels are a "step in the right direction." But, he adds, the labels don't communicate anything. "They don't use the word 'benefits.'"[67] It is likely that CEI's campaign will continue.

Other Media Gimmicks

Throughout 1995, the CEI used other press gimmicks, some more successful than others. When the FDA proposed to regulate tobacco as a drug, the CEI petitioned the agency to regulate coffee, colas, and other beverages as drugs as well. Kazman called it a "semi-parody" of the FDA for trying to classify cigarettes as a drug and indeed said in its letter to the FDA that it didn't "wish to see this petition granted."[68] The focus was not on drug approvals or off-label uses, but the effort continued to place the FDA in a negative light. CEI called a press conference, and got some media "hits." Knight-Ridder moved a story on its wires that dismissed CEI's petition as a "political protest," and called the CEI an anti-government-regulation think tank "substantially funded by the tobacco industry."[69] (Kazman says money from tobacco companies has never approached even half of CEI's budget.) The media failed to make the connection between the "protest" and CEI's larger objectives of undermining the FDA.

CEI had better luck in August when it reported on a poll of oncologists it had commissioned. When asked what they thought of the FDA and its advertising restrictions for off-label drug uses, three-fourths of the oncologists concluded that the FDA's approval process was too slow; nearly two-thirds said that the FDA's approval process had hurt their ability to care for patients; and more than 40 percent reported that favorable media treatment of FDA commissioner David Kessler contributed to the public's lack of understanding of the human costs associated with slow drug approvals.[70]

The poll results cycled through the conservative press. James Bovard cited the poll in a September *Washington Times* op-ed,[71] and Sen. Connie Mack, a Florida Republican, issued a press release trumpeting the poll. Mack had introduced legislation to lift restrictions on off-label drug uses. In an October editorial, the *Washington Times* called the poll results "remarkable."[72] Sam Kazman talked about the poll on KCBS radio news in San Francisco and on CNN.[73] In December, an op-ed in the *Wall Street Journal* by John Berlau, a policy analyst at

Consumer Alert (a free-market consumer group), attacked the FDA for its position opposing off-label drug uses. He cited CEI's poll.[74] In his lengthy op-ed in a December issue of the *Washington Times*, Doug Bandow, a senior fellow at the Cato Institute, described the results of the poll as "astounding."[75] Over a three-year period, CEI sources were quoted more than 300 times in various media giving their views on drug approvals or on the FDA's regulation of tobacco.[76] The mainstream media generally give short shrift to "inside the Beltway" topics involving the FDA. Given that such items, if they show up at all, are usually news fillers, the breadth and depth of the coverage accorded to the efforts of CEI and other think tanks pushing their anti-regulatory agendas was astonishing.

Passage of the Bill

How the conservative think-tank network built support for weakening the FDA illustrates the twin strategies described in chapter 1: moving mass opinion and neutralizing elite opinion. While media gimmicks helped cast doubt on the agency among the public, in the end, neutralizing elite opinion and working Capitol Hill made the real difference. It was not public outcry that stripped the FDA of some of its power, but legwork in legislative offices that softened up Congress for the changes the coalition wanted to make. Edward Hudgins, director of regulatory studies for Cato, explained the strategy as it applied to FDA reform: "Our main audience is the educated and informed policy maker." He said at one time Cato "tended to downplay Congress. We thought we had to affect opinion more broadly to affect change. But if you affect the ideas of opinion leaders and policy people, it will bring about permanent change."[77]

Both CEI and Cato commissioned Robert Higgs, research director of The Independent Institute, a libertarian think tank based in Oakland, California, to write lengthy papers on the FDA. The CEI paper was called "How FDA Is Causing a Technological Exodus"; the Cato paper, "Wrecking Ball: FDA Regulation of Medical Devices." Both papers made their way to the offices of former Senator Nancy Landon Kassebaum, whose Labor and Human Resources Committee was writing legislation to reform the FDA. Many of the provisions in a bill Kassebaum drafted mirrored the coalition's goals.[78] The Cato Institute also circulated its "Handbook for Congress," which argued for getting the government out of the drug-approval process and turning the task over to private business. The handbook declared that the stakes were high: "FDA reform is truly a matter of life and death not only for America's biotechnology industry but for the billions of people around the world who wait and hope for cures and better treatments for major illnesses."[79] In other words, changing the drug-approval process was as much an attempt to safeguard and increase biotech profits as it ostensibly was to help sick people.

Dr. Robert Goldberg, a senior research fellow at Brandeis University, wrote the FDA section. He had written several other anti-FDA articles, including an op-ed for the *Wall Street Journal* in the fall of 1996 and a lengthy piece in *Regulation,* published by the American Enterprise Institute.[80] Hudgins described Goldberg's role: "We try to keep a stable of academics to write things for us." Goldberg, he said, is a "good guy, and I try to use him as much as I can."[81]

In early 1996, Kassebaum's committee reported out a bill that would begin to "reform" FDA, and in mid-March, ABC's *Nightline* devoted a program to FDA drug lag. Taking the side of the anti-FDA forces, Cokie Roberts, the show's hostess, began with a sweeping generalization. She claimed that "enough people" could not get medical devices they needed, had left the country to get them, and were now bringing "the problem to the attention of the U.S. Congress."

The show also featured ABC's medical editor, Dr. Timothy Johnson. He reported that an Indiana company making heart stents to open blocked arteries could sell its products in Europe, but noted that "U.S. approval will likely be years away." Johnson could have asked some basic questions, such as: When did the company apply to FDA? How long did it take the FDA to respond to the initial application? What was the response? Was the data sufficient? Did the company have to do additional testing and supply more supporting data? What was the company's response? Did it delay submitting additional data? If he did ask, he did not report the answers. Nor did Johnson raise the important issue that Thomas Moore noted was missing from the debate: the efficacy and proper testing of drugs and devices for safety, and how such testing applied to the heart stent that the show focused on.

Johnson also promoted a solution: Take the responsibility and authority away from FDA, and allow outside companies to certify medical devices. He advocated a minimal role for the FDA: supervising the private companies that would actually certify the medical devices. That was one objective advanced by some of the think tanks and biotechnology firms.

The program did give a voice to others. One speaker was Jeffrey Eisenach, who headed Newt Gingrich's Progress &

Freedom Foundation, which the program identified as a conservative think tank that favors government deregulation. The program didn't tell viewers that biotechnology firms and drug manufacturers had given nearly half a million dollars to the foundation to lobby for a proposal to curb the FDA's powers. Dr. Sidney Wolfe, director of Public Citizen's Health Research Group, got one soundbite to offer an opposing viewpoint. The program did feature an FDA spokesman. Every time he raised the issue of efficacy, ABC interviewers tried to neutralize his remarks.[82]

In late July of 1996, Public Citizen released a fifty-three-page report, "A Million for Your Thoughts: The Industry-funded Campaign Against the FDA by Conservative Think Tanks." The report discussed the $3.5 million given between 1992 and 1995 to seven conservative think tanks by drug and medical-device manufacturers, biotechnology firms, tobacco companies, and the corporate foundations connected to all of them. Recipients included The Heritage Foundation, the Cato Institute, the Washington Legal Foundation, the Competitive Enterprise Institute, and the Progress & Freedom Foundation. The report tried to set the record straight about the inaccurate and misleading information that had made its way into the media.[83]

Public Citizen issued a press release in late July, which read: "By relying on industry-funded misinformation in crafting FDA legislation, Congress may well threaten the lives and well-being of millions of Americans."[84] The news media didn't bite. Health Line picked up the story, and there was an item in the AP/*Richmond Times-Dispatch*,[85] an item in the *National Law Journal,* and one in the *Market Letter.* Attempts to find out from Public Citizen why its report fell on deaf ears were fruitless. A spokesperson said: "The report speaks for itself. No one has questioned the accuracy of it."[86]

Epitomizing the right wing's knack for striking back quickly, CEI announced the results of a new medical specialists' poll on the same day Public Citizen sent out its press release. This time CEI reported what cardiologists thought of the FDA. The findings conveyed a message similar to the one found in the poll of oncologists. This time CEI found that 57 percent of the cardiologists surveyed believed that delays in drug approvals result in patient deaths, and 67 percent said they opposed FDA restrictions on off-label drug uses. The press release took a swipe at Public Citizen: "FDA reform is frequently attacked as a pet project of big business that will allegedly open the door to snake oil remedies. This characterization is wrong. As these polls demonstrate, for many medical specialists, fighting heart disease and cancer can often mean fighting FDA. If this isn't a public health problem in need of reform, what is?"[87]

CNN and Reuters picked up the CEI story, but for the most part it did not fare much better in the media than the report from Public Citizen.[88] CEI's Julie DeFalco responded with an op-ed in the *Washington Times* on August 15 denouncing Public Citizen, defending CEI's funding, and promoting the results of CEI's two polls of medical specialists.[89] It didn't matter that CEI's latest poll got little press pickup. CEI's quick response had neutralized Public Citizen's report. Perhaps by now the media were not interested in the FDA, or they had already come to believe that the kind of reform now advocated by conservative Republicans was necessary. Perhaps reporters thought they had written all there was to write in 1995 when many media outlets did acknowledge that right-wing think tanks were attacking the FDA. "The think tanks created a context in which they permitted the industry to come along in 1997 and portray the legislation as a moderate consensus approach," says Public Citizen's Maura Kealy. "The right wing softened the way so that an extremely dangerous bill designed to maximize profits at the expense of public health could pass."[90]

Shortly before the bill whizzed through the Senate, the FDA had ordered the recall of two popular diet drugs, fenfluramine and dexfenfluramine. When taken with the drug phentermine this combination was known as *fen-phen*. It turned out that two of these drugs damaged heart valves in some patients, and the FDA ordered manufacturers to recall them. The FDA had approved the use of the drugs separately for very obese patients, but had not approved their use in combination.

Nevertheless, doctors and diet clinics had begun prescribing the drug combo to broaden its use by those who were slightly overweight. This expanded off-label use, not incidentally, also boosted the bottom lines of the pharmaceutical companies that marketed the drugs.

The media hyped the fen-phen story. It offered drama, the specter of people being harmed, and a whiff of wrongdoing. A few media reports did note the link between fen-phen and the pending FDA legislation, which would allow drug companies to advertise and promote off-label uses, perhaps paving the way for another fen-phen disaster.

George Strait mentioned the connection on *ABC World News Tonight*. The segment featured Dr. Arnold Relman, the former editor of the *New England Journal of Medicine,* who cogently cut through the issue. "I don't see how this helps the health of the American people, protects them in any way, does anything good for the medical profession or for patients. As far as I can see, the only winners in this bill are the drug industry."[91] The *New York Times* ran an op-ed by Frank Clemente of Public Citizen pointing out the irony between fen-phen and the bill awaiting passage.[92] Several newspapers published editorials decrying attempts to weaken the FDA. Most news reporters, however, ignored the issue, buying into what had become conventional Washington wisdom that the FDA bill represented "moderate consensus." By the time any news accounts or editorials appeared, the FDA overhaul was a done deal—important interest groups had reached agreement. Even if every paper in the country had connected all the dots, it would not have changed the Congressional outcome.

For its part, the public scarcely knew what was going on. The *Washington Post* opined: "Despite months of mostly reasonable compromise, the FDA bill, for one, limps into home plate as a measure that in many small ways curbs and weakens the agency's oversight. It's hard to see the groundswell driving this endless exercise."[93] Neither the *Post* nor other media organizations had looked very hard.

The goal set by the Competitive Enterprise Institute three years earlier—providing the "intellectual and moral cover needed to advance into hostile policy terrain"—had been realized.

Media inattention to such a serious public-health issue raises questions about the old journalistic model and how it can and should respond to sustained, well-funded lobbying efforts by right-wing think tanks. Those groups are able to come back again and again with new "information"— another poll, another study, another press release—to keep an issue fresh and alive.

A good example was the "Go Away Party" CEI threw when David Kessler left the FDA in 1997. CEI celebrated with yet another report showing how the FDA "continues to prevent life saving therapies from coming to this country."[94] The report singled out particular drugs and medical devices, and got some coverage in *Bioworld Today,* the *Durham Herald Sun,* ABC Radio News, and WBZ-AM in Boston. The report offered reporters another chance to see who was behind the movement to reform the FDA, but they showed little zest for evaluating whether or not CEI's claims were true. Such claims might have sparked some media interest, especially after similar assertions about other drugs and devices made by the Washington Legal Foundation two years earlier were shown to be false or deceptive.

When the president finally signed the FDA modernization act in late November, the *New York Times,* the country's paper of record, carried a story in the back of the A section. The story was mostly speculation about who was going to replace Kessler. It quoted the president: "The FDA has always set the gold standard for consumer safety. Today it wins a gold medal for leading the way into the future." The story concluded that the new law would "allow drugs to be approved faster and expand access to drugs and therapies while F.D.A. approval was still pending."[95] From this story, a reader would never know what the new law was all about or how it came to be.

In 1995, Sidney Wolfe told a House subcommittee: "The

American public is not likely to tolerate any weakening of the FDA's regulatory authority or reduction in funding which . . . will reduce the safety of the food supply or worsen the safety of drugs and devices."[96] In retrospect, Wolfe's comments were naive and far off the mark. Congress significantly weakened the FDA, and the public hardly uttered a murmur. The drug and device industry had won the propaganda campaign waged on their behalf by the conservative think tanks.

Aftermath

In CEI's December 1997 newsletter, policy analyst Julie DeFalco complained: "We all had great expectations for a reform bill that would fundamentally change the FDA's relationship with patients and doctors. . . . The 'FDA Modernization and Accountability Act of 1997' is not the best of laws, it's not the worst either . . . it is unlikely that this Act will bring the great benefits to patients promised by Congress, the President, and the drug and medical device industries."[97]

"The issue of victim drug lag has gone up in a political sense," Sam Kazman says. "We're still looking for a politician who will make a cause out of it."[98] Before Christmas in 1997, the *Washington Times* took up the cause again with an editorial rebuking the FDA for its tardy approval of the Sensor Pad to detect breast lumps. The editorial said that Canada has authorized the marketing of the pad "in just 30 days"—a "fact" shown to be false two years earlier. The editorial also cited CEI's 1995 poll of oncologists.[99]

CEI commissioned a third poll in 1998, this time asking neurologists and neurosurgeons what they thought of the FDA and its drug approvals. Sixty-seven percent agreed that

94

the FDA was too slow in approving new drugs and medical devices, 58 percent agreed that the extra time it takes for the FDA to approve drugs and medical devices costs lives by forcing people to go without potentially beneficial therapies, and 80 percent said that the FDA's approval process has hurt their ability to treat patients with the best possible care at least once.[100] That poll, too, circulated in the media. The *Washington Times, Barron's,* and the *Augusta* (Georgia) *Chronicle,* for example, published editorials mentioning the poll.[101]

All of CEI's polls, clever gimmicks to support the group's position, were based on biased questions that would make most social scientists cringe. They didn't, for example, ask physicians if the FDA's regulations ever helped them treat patients or prevent their patients from receiving harmful or dangerous drugs. In the survey of neurologists, CEI asked if the FDA was too slow in approving drugs and devices, and if the time it took to approve drugs forced people to go without therapies. It didn't ask if the time it took to approve drugs helped prevent harmful drugs from reaching the market, an equally important consideration. The premise in all three polls was that the FDA was bad and slowed down the approval of life-saving drugs, but media stories never delved into the bias that was evident.

The newsletter *Inside Washington's FDA Week* came close, noticing that the neurologists' poll did not ask questions about whether the FDA modernization act had improved doctors' ability to provide care—something a more neutral poll would have done. A CEI spokesman told the newsletter it did not address the effects of the law because it did not think the law did much to speed up drug approvals and that the group's polling firm counseled that asking questions about the law would make the findings inaccurate.[102] In other words, if the neurologists had said something positive about the law, it might have made it more difficult for CEI to squeeze news value out of the poll and sustain media interest in its cause.

In 1998, stories also surfaced about drugs that were being recalled because the FDA detected serious problems with their safety. During the fiscal year that ended in June 1998, five pharmaceuticals—the diet drugs Redux and Pondimin; Seldane, an antihistamine; Posicor, a blood-pressure medication; and Duract, an anti-inflammatory—were recalled. That was the worst recall record since the Kefauver amendments were passed in 1962.[103]

Serious questions have been raised about Rezulin, a diabetes drug that has resulted in thirty-three deaths. The *Los Angeles Times* pointed out that the FDA had dismissed concerns raised by veteran medical officers about the drug's association with liver injuries; failed to require physicians to conduct liver tests on patients receiving the drug; and did not prevent Warner-Lambert, the manufacturer, from advertising seriously misleading safety claims.[104]

Not all of the recalls can be attributed to the aftereffects of the 1997 law. Some drugs had been approved long before the act was passed. Nevertheless, years of relentless pressure on the agency for speedy approvals has begun to take its toll. Public Citizen's Health Research Group surveyed FDA scientists and asked whether the agency had inappropriately approved some two dozen new drugs; 19 percent said that they had.[105]

No one knows what will happen when the changes called for in the new legislation begin to affect the public. Only time will tell if the continuing campaign by the right-wing think tanks will pay off for them and their funders and whether public health will suffer the consequences. "The real question is are we getting sufficient testing done," says Thomas Moore. "There are signs, evidence that drugs that need more testing or shouldn't have been approved are reaching the market. Speed can be a mistake."[106]

4

*Masking Ideology as Research:
Bringing Down Head Start*

"One difference between Cato and Heritage is style. Heritage focuses on the short term, Cato focuses on the long term. We tend to do more booklike publications in depth and more basic research."
    —Edward Hudgins,
        Director of regulatory studies, The Cato Institute[1]

No issue better illustrates the Cato Institute philosophy about basic research than its 1993 assault on Head Start, one of the crown jewels of Lyndon Johnson's Great Society. Over its thirty-four-year history, Head Start has served almost 17 million preschoolers. Its mission through the years has remained unchanged. The program, aimed at disadvantaged children, tries to build their sense of dignity, self-confidence, and self worth by focusing on physical health and social and emotional development. Head Start also focuses on "improving the child's mental processes and skills, with particular attention to conceptual and verbal skills."[2]

Though the program enjoys popular support, Head Start has taken its share of criticism, some thoughtful and justified. Not all of its 43,000 classrooms have offered top-notch services. Some teachers are poorly trained and poorly paid, and child development experts now believe that interventions should occur even earlier than those provided by Head Start. Some evidence has surfaced that short-term benefits provided by the program may dissipate over time unless children continue to receive high-quality education in their later school years.

Inadequate funding has at times plagued the program, and lack of money along with increased enrollment have at times resulted in poor quality at some of the centers. Throughout the 1980s, enrollment increased; so did absolute dollars poured into the program.[3] But not enough money came in, and the average expenditure per child actually decreased. Head Start has never reached all of the estimated two million children who are eligible for the program. Furthermore, some of the centers suffered from poor program oversight and control, and many center administrators lacked adequate training and credentials.

Nevertheless, Head Start has enjoyed widespread popular support from many quarters—from Democrats and Republicans, from minority communities and from the public at large. For nearly two generations, Head Start has been hailed as a model program that provides some basic medical care, including immunizations, and tries to ensure that poor children gain appropriate skills to move ahead. Few people question its raison d'être or the money spent on the program, which has sometimes been called America's most successful educational experiment.

Shortly after taking office and responding to the need to improve the quality of Head Start sites, President Clinton signaled his intention to pump more money into the program, then costing the federal government some $2.2 billion a year.[4]

In late 1992, Cato, whose libertarian philosophy is to get government out of people's lives and protect only life, liberty, and property, released Policy Analysis No. 187[5]: "Caveat Emptor: The Head Start Scam." The report, a seventeen-page, single-spaced analysis, attacked the Head Start program head-on. Implicit and explicit in the pages was the argument that the billions of dollars the federal government had poured into Head Start were a waste of money. "A mix of private-sector, nonprofit church, community group, and extended family providers is a better way to provide such care for children, poor or not,"[6] the report argued, and concluded that a "better approach would be to convert federal money now committed to Head Start into vouchers or tax relief to give parents the opportunity to send their children to private or parochial schools in their communities."[7]

Cato's attack on Head Start was emblematic of the strategy used not only by Cato but by other right-wing think tanks that dress up ideology as objective evaluation. These organizations develop and disseminate "research" that redirects and even misuses available evidence for conservative ideological ends. Cato's analysis was an attempt to discredit Head Start by focusing on its weaknesses and offering the right wing's solutions for fixing them—in this case, eliminate the program. The Cato report, for instance, appeared about the same time as a study from the Office of the Inspector General, which was critical of the quality of some programs.

Cato's attack also exemplified the media's gullibility, intellectual laziness, and eagerness to run with a story without re-searching what was behind it. The media gave a massive amount of attention to Cato's one-sided analysis, failed to do its own digging to verify its claims, and allowed Cato to por-tray Head Start in a way that was both incomplete and mis-leading.

Seeding the Ground with Bad Research

The tone of Policy Analysis No. 187 was also classic of the right wing's rhetorical style of unbridled scorn for federal pro-grams. Laced with words such as "hype," "myth," "public relations triumph," and "slick salesmanship," the report stated early on: "Head Start's impressive public relation triumph should surprise no one . . . Head Start's sales pitch works wonderfully . . . Head Start's hucksters, all smiles and prom-ises, have sold the public on a shiny prototype that bears little resemblance to what will actually be provided and, upon closer examination, is an empty shell with nothing under the hood."[8] That language fortified the title of the report.

The same could have been said about Cato's analysis. A careful reader should have discerned that the think tank's "re-search" was transparent and the report itself intellectually dis-honest. Only three citations could be construed as major reports on the Head Start program.[9] The report cited articles in the popular press, such as *Time,* the *Christian Science Monitor, Newsweek,* and specialized periodicals such as *American Demo-graphics* and *NEA Today* for details that boosted the points it wanted to make. It cited a *Newsweek* story, for example, laud-ing the publication for "breaking a virtual 'code of silence' among the major media" in daring to publish a critical story about Head Start. *Newsweek* reported on a Chicago study that claimed that gains made in the Head Start program do not last. The Chicago study showed that while only 62 percent of the participating students graduated, compared to the national average of 80 percent, the graduation rate among Head Start children had improved relative to a control group of poor children. Cato inferred from this, and noted in its report, that the long-term impact of the Chicago program was "nevertheless disappointing."[10]

The Cato analysis attacked statements made by "Head Start boosters" for saying that the program had fallen short of its potential because of federal neglect and budget cuts. It also contended that the 1992 appropriation of $2.2 billion represented a 70 percent increase over the 1981 budget.[11]

To bolster its conclusions and give the paper an aura of credibility, Cato peppered its analysis with carefully selected critical comments by influential experts from the realm of child development—Harvard psychologist Jerome Kagan and behaviorial psychologist Sandra Scarr. The report took snatches of their criticisms, ignored their solutions, and substituted Cato's own prescriptions as a response to their critiques.

The report argued that "it became apparent that children's minds are so unique, and personal traits so determined by heredity and idiosyncratic relationships between particular parents and children that researchers could no longer defend their limitless faith in the efficacy of intervention."[12] He then quoted Kagan as saying he was a political liberal who had been critical of the role of biology and celebrated the role of the environment but was now working in the opposite camp because "I was dragged there by my data."[13] Kagan later said, "the author took some of my comments out of context and used them for his own benefit." He noted that "where [Policy Analysis No. 187] distorts is to assume that Head Start can't help some children. If you restrict yourselves to good quality programs, then the data do show good results."[14]

Cato's analysis portrayed Scarr as an enemy of Head Start, quoting her as saying, "There is quite a mystique in our culture about the importance of early intervention . . . there is no evidence [for it] whatever." The report said Scarr and other child-development experts "clearly reject the notion that 'investing' our hopes and tax dollars in preschool education programs such as Head Start will make our social ills go away."[15] In fact, in 1993, Scarr (along with sixteen other scholars in the field of child development) signed a letter to Congress endorsing the president's proposals to strengthen and fully fund Head Start.[16]

The analysis did not present a fuller description of what Scarr thought of the Head Start program or how it should be improved. Instead readers got Cato's conclusion two sentences later. "It's the public schools that must change. Head Start is neither a necessary nor a sufficient condition for helping poor children succeed."[17]

The first paragraph of Policy Analysis No. 187, which described various victories in establishing educational vouchers and school choice across the country, articulated the report's apparent goal: to make readers believe that Head Start should be scrapped and replaced with a system of grants or vouchers that would allow poor families to send their children to private or parochial schools. The second to the last paragraph brought the point home. The government wouldn't necessarily spend less, under Cato's reasoning, but would simply shift money to the private educational market, giving private and parochial schools a chance to benefit from government largesse.[18]

The report noted that a voucher system "would be a much better 'public investment' than extending the federal government's reach further into the lives of preschool children."[19] Despite its advocacy of vouchers, the paper presented no evidence or research to support its contention that vouchers for older children are a better approach than early intervention for young ones. It didn't promote vouchers for preschoolers, which might have been a reasonable extension of Cato logic, but instead offered another "solution" for preschoolers (in addition to ending Head Start)—the elimination of regulations that now govern day care in most localities.[20]

Cato argued that "local and state regulations of employees, staff-child ratios, services, insurance, and amenities all significantly increase the per child cost of preschool and child care significantly. [sic]"[21] What regulations did Cato have in mind—those that ensure adequate space, require enough adults to care for children, mandate health screenings for child-care workers? Which amenities did it want to eliminate—playground equipment, lunches and snacks, juice and milk? The report didn't say.

It did, however, posit reasons why the program should disappear:

- Evidence used to promote Head Start came from programs that were not Head Start programs.
- Heredity so strongly determines behavior that early intervention is a waste of time and makes little difference.

• Medical, nutritional, and educational services, while of
some immediate benefit to poor children, are better provided by the private sector.

The analysis also noted that academic training for young children is not advisable. While it didn't expressly say that Head
Start was promoting academic subjects, it offered that implication by stringing together seemingly related points. For example, it stated that "there is no evidence that formal centers
or preschools necessarily provide better care for children than
informal centers and homes." In the next sentence, the paper
quoted a professor of early childhood education at the University of Illinois saying that academic training was not a good
idea for preschoolers.[22] A casual reader could easily construe
that Head Start was teaching algebra to four-year-olds when it
does not. But the implications of that passage offered yet another reason why Head Start had to go.

The Press Takes the Bait

Over the next several months, Cato's report took on a life of
its own as it traveled through the media. The press reported
Cato's "research" and conclusions with scarcely a nod to objective analysis and comment. Instead of doing its own investigations of the Head Start program, examining its successes
and failures, and what was necessary to make it work better,
the press let Cato frame the story as well as the solution—that
the program was a failure and should be junked. Without
questioning the report or its premise, reporters and columnists
built their stories around Cato's attack, allowing the think

tank to advance its agenda of getting the government out of people's lives.

The journey of Policy Analysis No. 187 through the media began in mid-December of 1992 with a Cato press release that advocated the end of Head Start. The press release carried a quote from the report that the program was "neither a necessary nor a sufficient condition for helping poor children succeed," and it made a pitch for vouchers or tax relief for parents to send children to private or parochial schools.[23]

Two months later, the report began its travels in earnest with publication of a *Wall Street Journal* op-ed that appeared shortly after Clinton announced his intention to seek more money for Head Start. The op-ed was written by John Hood, the author of Policy Analysis No. 187. The op-ed identified Hood as research director of the John Locke Foundation, a state-policy think tank in Raleigh, North Carolina. In the op-ed, Hood gave a shortened version of his report, arguing that "if we're all going to be good 'public investors,' we have to examine the rate of return of various options—Head Start vs. school vouchers, for example, and set priorities."[24]

Hood is now president of the John Locke Foundation. He is not a journalist nor an expert in child development. Nor is the John Locke Foundation a contributor to the child-development literature.[25] The foundation works mostly on state fiscal matters. Nevertheless, Hood's detour into the world of child development earned him instant status as an expert in early childhood education. The media accorded Hood expert credibility he didn't merit and gave his report credence it didn't deserve. Hood later told a researcher for a Harvard School of Public Health project on science, technology, and the news media that he was "essentially a reporter" and was "in no way more qualified to check these things out than a reporter." He said he was reporting on what other psychologists had found and never intended for the report to be perceived as an academic study. When the Harvard investigator asked Hood to describe his research methods, he replied: "I looked in the various indexes that are available to any college student."[26]

If Hood was acting as a journalist and not an expert in child development, it was not apparent to many of his colleagues in journalism. Hood said: "There were reporters who originally called and they'd say, 'you did a study of what program?' or 'You run what preschool?'"[27] For one of its backgrounders for reporters, the Education Writers Association, a professional organization for some 800 journalists covering education, listed Hood as a key figure in the Head Start debate and someone whom reporters could turn to for assistance and comment. When the Harvard researcher questioned Lisa Walker, executive director of the association, about Hood's credentials, she explained: "I don't know what his background was. He had recently been writing things in the paper about issues relating to Head Start, so I had pulled his name out of other citations. And most likely the reason I put him down there is that we're almost always criticized from the right for not having enough breadth of opinion in our backgrounders, so I've been making a concerted effort more recently to also include conservatives. I think that reporters need to know the range of opinions whether or not they're necessarily supported."[28]

On the same day Hood's op-ed appeared, the *Washington*

Post also ran a news story trumpeting Hood's study. The *Post* story was headlined "As Politicians Expand Head Start, Experts Question Worth, Efficiency." In the third paragraph, Hood was the first "expert" quoted. He said: "Politicians always seem to be the last people to catch on to academic trends." The *Post* story identified Hood as the author of a 1992 Cato Institute study that showed new research is "raising doubts about the efficacy of Head Start." The paragraph implied that Hood was an academic and that his report revealed new research about the program.[29] The *Post* reporter apparently didn't read the report critically, or discover the holes in it which might have been worth commenting on, or which might have prompted her to question the report's premise to begin with.

Nevertheless, the story moved on the *Post* newswire and several papers across the country picked it up. When the *Post* story reached the *Phoenix Gazette*, the headline became "Academics, others question effectiveness of Head Start." As in the *Washington Post* version, Hood was the first person quoted, which implied that he was an academic and that the Cato Institute was an authority on child development.[30]

A few weeks later, the *Macon Telegraph* carried the scholarly implication a step further. In an editorial "Time for a Colder, Closer Look at Head Start," the paper opined, "it may be useful to consider critical reviews of its academic effectiveness. It is possible on the Cato evidence that Head Start has been overpraised, oversold, overfunded, and under criticized."[31] What "evidence" were editorial writers referring to? Cato, of course, presented no scholarly research evidence of its own; that is, no study with control groups and peer review that might make its conclusions credible. Instead it offered as "evidence" out-of-context quotes with Cato's conclusions neatly woven into other people's thoughts about the program. Apparently that was good enough for the editorial board of the *Macon Telegraph.*

Cato's "expertise" in child development was never questioned. In fact, many press accounts did not even mention Cato's ideological credentials. They presented Cato as simply another research group, of which there are hundreds in Washington. But without some description or characterization of those organizations, the reader has a hard time decoding their messages. The *Washington Post* story, for example, merely mentioned "Cato Institute" without telling readers where Cato stood on the ideological spectrum. The *Chicago Tribune* and the *Detroit News,* as well as smaller papers like the *Lubbock Avalanche-Journal* and the *Youngstown Vindicator,* didn't identify Cato either.

Detroit News editorial writer Bill Johnson simply called Cato a "Washington-based research organization." In the first paragraph of a column titled "Claims of Head Start's Success May Be Exaggerated," he set out a premise that echoed Cato's. "No doubt more child-oriented programs that teach social skills to disadvantaged, at-risk preschoolers could have long-term payoffs," he wrote. "But the investment is unwise until and unless Head Start's effectiveness is confirmed."[32]

The Harvard researcher later questioned Johnson about his column. He told her he rejected the belief that Head Start can have a positive, lasting impact on children and said that the program was "primarily a babysitting service for a lot of mothers." As for the Cato report, he said it was probably the first comprehensive study of the program. Johnson said he knew nothing about Hood or his background but that in his eyes, Cato was a "credible organization," so he believed its analysis.[33]

Other columnists also found Cato's analysis believable. Linda Seebach, a columnist for the *Los Angeles Daily News,* began her column on Head Start this way: "Head Start is a waste of time and money, and a great many people associated with the program have known that for a long time." The column ended with the observation that Cato had demolished the arguments advanced by Head Start proponents that money spent on the program means less spent later on social pathology.[34]

Other papers, including the *Baltimore Sun,* published Seebach's column. Cathy Ridenour, policy chairperson for the Western Maryland Child Care Resource Center, challenged Seebach's research in the *Sun* several weeks later. She examined some of the same studies Seebach used for her column and discovered that Seebach had "only used the negative sides of the stories." Ridenour concluded: "Maybe next time before someone tries to put down Project Head Start, he or she will research both sides of the fence."[35]

Reporters writing about the Cato report didn't do that. They did, however, quote Dr. Edward Zigler, a professor of psychology at Yale University, one of Head Start's founders, and still one of its biggest boosters. But reporters almost uniformly cast Zigler in the role of a supporting critic of Head Start by misreading his appraisals of the program. They took his quotes out of context, often making it appear that he was in full alignment with Cato's views. For example, the *Wash-*

111

ington Post story quoted Zigler: "If 30 percent [of the centers] closed down, there would be no great loss. Why put a lot of kids in a program that is no good? Until the program has reached a certain minimum level of quality, they shouldn't put one more kid in it."[36] The *Post* story and others did not expand on what Zigler meant by quality or amplify what he would do to improve the program.

Zigler's quotes offered the chance to look closely at Head Start to see how it could be improved. Instead they were used to support Cato's position. Zigler's criticisms were intended to improve the quality of the program, not destroy it, but they didn't come across that way. "The model is absolutely terrific," he later said. "But the program around the country is not uniformly of high quality. The media made it sound like all the programs are bad. There's no story in saying these programs are terrific."[37] By quoting Zigler in the manner they did without further discussion, the media unwittingly supported Cato's agenda: Eliminate its funding and starve the program so it ultimately fails. "There was a feeling among the right wing that if they bring Head Start down, all other programs will fall with it," Zigler said.[38]

Zigler wrote a twenty-eight-page rebuttal to Hood. In it, he charged that: "Hood's failure to research even the basic facts of Head Start's birth shows a lack of knowledge about the program he is criticizing." Zigler called Hood's analysis "poorly researched" and attacked Hood's conclusions that a competitive marketplace can provide more efficient child care and preschool education.[39]

"To end a critique of early childhood intervention with a recommendation for parental choice of supplementary care and nursery school is a non sequitur," Zigler wrote. "Standard preschool education programs and the mixed system of child care do not provide the comprehensive services that define Head Start. Nor are health care, parental empowerment, and family support easily obtained in the fragmented system of social service delivery without the help of a coordinator—a role filled by Head Start."[40]

Zigler sent his rebuttal to the Clinton administration and to Capitol Hill staff. He said he didn't see any need to take his comments to the press.[41] If Zigler had given the media his report and explained how Head Start could fulfill its potential, perhaps coverage would have been less one-sided.

Maybe Zigler didn't think he had to sell his ideas; many progressives don't. Instead they rely on the implicit correctness of their cause to make their case. In this age of slick salesmanship by the right wing, that is not enough.

Aftermath

Cato did not succeed this time in bringing down Head Start. The Head Start program is small potatoes in the federal budget compared to hundreds of billions spent for Social Security and Medicare. According to Hood, Cato worked at getting media coverage for his analysis, but the think tank soon turned its attention to Social Security, pouring millions of dollars into a campaign to privatize the system—a campaign that is beginning to make inroads into the public's thinking about that program. Privatizing Social Security potentially offers a much bigger payoff for the right wing and its corporate allies than removing Head Start does, and it's easier to portray elderly people at the end of their lives as undeserving claimants on the

113

public funds than it is children. "If you savage Head Start, you savage children," says Helen Blank, director of child care at the Children's Defense Fund.[42]

But Head Start also had powerful protectors—the president of the United States and his wife. The Clintons intended to improve Head Start and remedy its shortcomings as soon as they arrived in Washington. Early on, Clinton announced that he planned to increase its budget to nearly $6 billion by 1997. Although the administration has fallen short of its goal, it has protected Head Start funding during the horse trading that occurs during budget negotiations. It has insisted on more money even when House Republicans have tried to cut Head Start appropriations. The $2.2 billion program that reached some 621,000 children when the Clintons came to the White House has now metamorphosed into a $4.7-billion program that touches the lives of some 822,000 youngsters.[43]

Congress has not only reauthorized the program but imposed requirements to upgrade the quality of the teachers and the programs. It has also enacted the Early Head Start program for younger children, an attempt to reach vulnerable children earlier in their development.

Cato's attack, however, did cause many of its longtime friends and supporters to take a second look and question the program. The National Head Start Association, the umbrella group for all the Head Start sites, began an intensive lobbying effort to keep a positive image of the program in front of politicians. It embarked on a drive to get every member of Congress to visit a program. "We said come in, see the books. If you have questions, come look for yourself," said Sarah Greene, the association's chief executive officer. "We had to start presenting position papers to show why Head Start worked—why it was an effective program."[44]

The Clintons saved Head Start, and Cato's attack withered largely because of the president's willingness to improve the program. But Cato, by its own admission, is in for the long haul. This time destroying Head Start wasn't worth the effort. But who is to say that Cato won't try again when Head Start's sugar daddy leaves office?

5

Advancing a Cause: Remaking Medicare

"Publicly funded political advocates rarely find themselves debating anyone who's privately funded. They are all supported by tax dollars. If their ideas are so compelling, let them go out in the marketplace, as Heritage does, and see if the public agrees with them enough to support them."[1]
— Kate O'Beirne,
former Vice President, The Heritage Foundation

In fall of 1997, at a symposium of American and Japanese journalists looking at aging in the twenty-first century, Robyn Stone, who had recently resigned her post as assistant secretary for Health and Human Services, chastised the American reporters in the audience: "What is amazing to me is that you have not picked up on probably the most significant story in aging since the 1960s and that is the passage of the Balanced Budget Act of 1997, which creates Medicare Plus Choice. This is the beginning of the end of entitlements for the Medicare program." The changes, Stone said, signaled a move toward a "defined contribution" program rather than a "defined benefit" plan with a predetermined set of benefits for everyone. The "legislation was so gently passed that nobody looked at the details."[2]

Robert Rosenblatt, a *Los Angeles Times* reporter who covers the aging beat, immediately challenged her. "It's not the beginning of the end of Medicare as we know it," he shot back. "It expands consumer choice."[3]

The Balanced Budget Act did expand the range of options Medicare beneficiaries have for covering their health-care expenses, but in this case, choice was a slippery concept. As Stone pointed out, "choice" could mean the end of Medicare as a universal social program that has paid the medical bills for millions of elderly men and women since 1965.

But during debate on the Balanced Budget Act, the press did little to help the public understand the far-reaching implications of provisions embedded deep in the legislation. The media had been so thoroughly sold on the mantra of choice peddled by right-wing think tanks and their allies in Congress that they missed the fundamental changes those groups were advancing.

The exchange between Stone and reporters illustrated the effectiveness of a three-year media campaign waged by The Heritage Foundation to reshape Medicare into a program where the government gives beneficiaries a set amount of money to buy their own coverage.

Employing a strategy that drew in allies and opinion leaders, bombarded the media with press releases, studies, and analyses, and strongly influenced what was written and aired, Heritage and its allies were able to impose their own prescription to finance health care for the elderly—a free market approach that shifts costs to beneficiaries. Heritage's solution is well on its way to becoming law, and other ideas have hardly been discussed, not because they don't have merit, but because they have effectively been shut out. "Heritage can take credit for showing what effective communications can do in controlling the debate," says Manhattan Institute president Larry Mone.[4]

Through sheer ideological exuberance, a slick public relations machine that conducted an effective educational campaign, and a very fat budget—more than $30 million— Heritage sowed the seeds in the Balanced Budget Act for converting Medicare from a social insurance program into a private insurance arrangement.

In the Balanced Budget legislation, Congress approved new options for beneficiaries that open the door to a voucher system akin to the one the government uses for its own employees, and not coincidentally the prototype marketed by Heritage. Heritage began selling the idea of a voucher-*cum*-choice model of health care in 1989 with a monograph called "A National Health System for America," which outlined how choice and competition would work. In 1992, at the beginning of the public conversation on health reform, Heritage embraced the Federal Employees Health Benefits Program (FEHBP) model and pushed the concept of a "Consumer Choice Health Plan," using ads placed in such publications as *Roll Call, The New Republic,* and *The American Spectator.* The ads sent this message: "If it's good enough for them [members of Congress], surely it's good enough for all Americans."[5]

The FEHBP model applied to Medicare allows the government to shrink its payments, thus shifting more of the cost to those who use the services. Beneficiaries, not the federal government, would bear a large burden for the escalating costs of medical care. The government would give an insurance company or a managed-care firm a fixed amount of money to provide benefits. If, over time, that payment was too small to provide the basic Medicare benefits, beneficiaries would have to pay the difference.

The FEHBP model potentially undermines the collective risk-sharing that makes Medicare work. If too many beneficiaries choose among the options and opt out of the traditional program, eventually only the sickest and hardest to insure will remain in Medicare's risk pool, making the program expensive and untenable. The premiums paid by healthy people who leave would go to insurance companies, doctors, and hospital organizations instead of subsidizing care for the sick. Large numbers of sick elderly people would be unable to shoulder the additional financial burden and would perhaps go without care.

Whether the FEHBP model would work for Medicare is open to question. In reality, there is little difference in premiums and benefits offered by insurers to federal employees. Federal employees are healthier and better educated than Medicare beneficiaries and are more likely to understand the differences that do exist. Nor is it clear that the FEHBP model would save the federal government money in the long run. The evidence that such a market-driven model will save money is "much disputed," says former Medicare administrator Bruce Vladeck. "No one has convinced any responsible actuary or economist that it will save substantial amounts of money. Over a reasonably long period of time, costs per beneficiary in FEHBP have risen at the same rate as Medicare costs. The only way to save the government money is to shift more cost to beneficiaries."[6]

In 1997, however, most of the media did not dwell on the long-range implications of an FEHBP-style Medicare. Nor did they focus on what was really at stake: whether health insurance for the elderly will be financed collectively through taxes paid by everyone and whether the elderly will bear the increasing cost of care themselves. When baby boomers retire, Medicare will have to support twice as many beneficiaries, and unless revenues go up, the program can't cover the increased costs. The press didn't discuss raising revenues, though. Instead it focused on short-term fixes aimed at cutting Medicare services. The media reported on a brief Congressional flirtation with raising the age of eligibility and increasing the premiums for Part B services, which cover physician and outpatient care.

They framed their stories and editorials as more of a dare to President Clinton to do the "right thing," which was to cut spending and make beneficiaries pay more. A column by *Washington Post* columnist David Broder was typical. The column appeared in several newspapers with headlines similar to this one from the *Austin American-Statesman:* "With a Little Courage, Clinton Can Make History with Medicare." Broder advocated raising the age of eligibility, and tried to make the case that this change plus charging the affluent higher premiums will pass only if Clinton "assures the members of the Republican majority that he will not use Medicare against them—as he did in 1996—and encourages reluctant House Democrats to embrace the Senate changes. History is knocking on Clinton's door. But so far, he is not answering."[7]

The accepted notion was that Medicare was in trouble, and that cuts could save it if politicians could muster the courage to make beneficiaries pay more. That was a simple story to report, much easier than deconstructing the implications of choice and telling beneficiaries, most of whom have never really understood how Medicare works, what kinds of complicated and inscrutable options Congress was about to thrust upon them.

In the end, Congress did slash spending by some $116 billion over five years (and by $394 billion over ten years), mostly through cuts in payments to providers. It also doubled Part B premiums for beneficiaries, from 526 dollars in 1998 to 1,025 dollars in 2005, a hefty increase considering that 54 percent of all beneficiaries have annual incomes under $15,000.[8] When Congress had finished, the increase, let alone its magnitude, was scarcely reported. "A lot of the changes were treated by the media as ho-hum, simply tweaking the Medicare program," says Marilyn Moon, an economist at The Urban Institute and a Medicare trustee. "They looked so much more moderate compared to 1995."[9]

The Reform Effort Begins

Medicare "reform" began its journey on February 15, 1995, when Heritage issued a committee brief, one of some 200 issue bulletins it sends out each year to convey its messages to members of Congress, editorial-page writers, columnists, and radio talk-show hosts.[10] This six-page document, titled, "A Special Report to the House Ways and Means Committee," set the agenda. Vice President Stuart Butler made a case for raising Part B premiums, offered several options, and emphasized that changes "should be taken in tandem with steps toward structural reform of the entire Medicare program." "The aim of the structural changes," he wrote, "should be a Medicare system in which retirees receive a contribution toward the cost of coverage (perhaps inversely related to income) which they may use to enroll in a plan of their choice."[11] The committee brief became a blueprint for re-shaping the program.

On the same day, Heritage sent out one of its red-bannered news releases. The release, based on the committee brief, noted that "structural reform is essential" and that it would involve "giving the elderly a fixed voucher—sometimes called a 'medicheck'—and then allowing the elderly to enroll in the type of plan they want, not the current highly regulated plan run from Washington."[12]

In early 1995, Heritage took its campaign to the backrooms of the Capitol. A few months later, it ginned up its public-marketing machine. Soon after the Medicare trustees released their annual report in April describing how Medicare's Part A trust fund, which pays hospital bills, would run out of money in 2002, the Heritage PR operation swung into action. On May 4, a news release headlined "Reform Medicare or Face Huge Tax Increases, Analyst Says" landed on journalists' desks.[13]

That the Hospital Trust Fund would run out of money after the turn of the century was no secret—or hot news for that matter. For several years, Medicare trustees had been predicting deficits and outlining increases in payroll taxes needed to cover them. The 1995 report restated the issues, but this time the report offered a convenient justification for Heritage and later the Republicans to "save" Medicare with their consumer-choice model. Increasing payroll taxes, or any new tax for that matter, as a solution was out of the question, and the Heritage propaganda arm made sure that taxes would never be seriously discussed.

The May 4 release mentioned the trustees' report and called for "massive reforms in the way medical benefits are delivered to the elderly."[14] With that release, Heritage sent along an F.Y.I., a PR device that succinctly sums up the think tank's point of view and pushes its solutions, whether the topic is Medicare, foreign trade policy, or taxes. Heritage also invited journalists and others to hear a lecture a few days later, with Rep. Bill Thomas, a California Republican, as the featured speaker. The subject: What It Takes to Reform Medicare.[15] The campaign to win the hearts and minds of the media had begun.

On May 12, Heritage reached the media big leagues, the *MacNeil/Lehrer NewsHour.* Robert MacNeil asked if Medicare could be cut back without hurting senior citizens. Patrick McGuigan, editorial-page editor of the *Daily Oklahoman,* promoted the Heritage agenda. He said that Heritage and others had "some serious ideas out there that would affect all aspects of health care, so maybe we ought to get those on the table now and see if there's market-oriented ways to do some of these same things."[16]

Although vouchers got some media attention, they did not become the big story. Instead, the Republican drive to cut $270 billion from Medicare gathered the headlines. Republicans needed the Medicare savings to fulfill a promise for a tax cut and a balanced budget in seven years. Throughout the year, the media conducted a prolonged dialogue on cuts—in reality a diversion that allowed Heritage to sell Congress on the idea of a defined contribution plan. The media dwelled on cuts; Heritage concentrated on more fundamental reform.

Republican pollster Frank Luntz set the stage. In May, Luntz conducted focus groups with the help of United Seniors Association, a right-wing organization for the elderly that was positioned as an alternative to AARP. The group gave cover to Republican efforts to transform Medicare, and later was to play an important role with the media when Heritage's ideas began to germinate.

Luntz learned that seniors did not value choice of healthcare plans as a high priority; seniors would not even consider changes in Medicare until they were convinced the system was going broke; and that no one believed Medicare would actually go bankrupt. So he designed a masterful strategy that did not dwell on choice, and fashioned the "correct" words and themes that would resonate with the elderly.[17]

In a communications memo sent to House Republicans, Luntz instructed them to:

- distribute a summary of the trustees report
- read to them word-for-word the most egregious conclusions
- tell them trustees include high-level Clinton administration officials and list them by name
- appear bipartisan
- tell them that your number-one priority is to "save Medicare"

Communications rules that apply in other situations don't apply in Medicare, Luntz cautioned. "Words are especially important, and setting the right tone at the outset is critical," he noted. "Saving, preserving, and strengthening Medicare" must be repeated, he instructed, adding that Republicans should not talk about "improving" Medicare. "When seniors hear the words 'improve' and 'Medicare' in the same sentence, they immediately think of lower deductibles, free prescription drugs, subsidized hearing aids and eyeglasses, cheaper

125

in-home care, and reductions in everything else they now have to pay for."[18]

The strategy worked. In a document called "Mandate for Leadership IV," distributed in 1997, Heritage boasted: "Over just a few weeks, the idea of a financial crisis in Medicare became accepted by an overwhelming majority of Americans."[19]

Politicians followed Luntz's script, and the media reported their lines. Representative Dan Miller, a Florida Republican, became a key spokesman. Early on, Miller appeared on CNN's *Inside Politics*: "First of all," he said, "we're not making cuts. We're going to be increasing spending on Medicare. Right now we're spending about forty-six hundred dollars for every person under the Medicare program. Our proposed plan is, say in the year 2002, we're going to spend about sixty-three hundred for everybody on Medicare, so we're going to be increasing the amount of spending."[20]

What Miller didn't say, and few in the media explained, was that slowing the rate of growth in the program was tantamount to a cut. The growing number of beneficiaries, advances in technology, and health-care inflation all increase the cost of Medicare. Slowing the growth rate so it doesn't keep pace with those changes effectively cuts the program (something Congress succeeded in doing with the Balanced Budget Act in 1997).

Media Critics Swing into Action

Throughout the summer, the media found itself engaged in a war of semantics over the word "cut," allowing Republicans to insist that they weren't cutting Medicare. Republican polls showed that the public reacted negatively when told that Republicans would cut Medicare. They reacted positively when told that spending would increase but at a slower rate. Nonetheless, if spending does not rise faster than inflation, it's a cut, but Republicans did not want journalists using that word. To police the way the media portrayed the Republican efforts in 1995, Brent Bozell's Media Research Center swung into action.

In June 1995, it fell to *MediaNomics*, one of the Center's publications, to sanction journalists every time they said the wrong thing. Over a fifteen-day period, Bozell kept score. *MediaNomics* reported that twelve stories referred to the Republican plan as a "cut," and said that six of those stories "repeated, without challenging, Democratic charges that Republicans wanted to cut Medicare to 'pay for' tax cuts for the wealthy."[21]

The newsletter criticized Linda Douglass of CBS for reporting that the senior citizens lobby had warned that the Republican budget will gut Medicare. It reprimanded Connie Chung of CBS for reporting that House and Senate GOP plans "call for deep cuts in Medicare and other programs."[22] Its sister publication, *Media Watch,* hit reporters for painting a "frightening picture of 'cuts'." It criticized *USA Today* for saying that Senator Pete Domenici's budget would "make huge cuts in Medicare and Medicaid." It clubbed *Newsweek*'s Tom Rosenstiel for saying Republicans "would slash funding for . . . medical care for the poor and elderly."[23]

MediaNomics also criticized reporters for talking to politicians instead of businessmen or conservative economists. The newsletter often listed conservative sources at the back of each issue, and instructed reporters to call those sources "for balance."

Bozell's newsletters were not all negative. They singled out certain reporters for praise—those whose work was compatible with the ideology of the Media Research Center. Lisa Myers of NBC was one of the favorites. "NBC's Lisa Myers also distinguished herself from the pack of network reporters by bringing up points others missed," *MediaNomics* noted. "In all three of Myers' stories, she referred to the Republican Medicare plan accurately as 'slowing its growth.' " The newsletter said that Myers was the only reporter to point out that the elderly are getting far more in benefits than they ever paid in taxes[24]—a statement demonstrating that Myers misunderstood the program.

Medicare is not an investment plan, enabling beneficiaries to withdraw in benefits the same amount they paid in premiums—a notion the right wing sometimes uses to discredit social insurance, particularly Social Security. Medicare is social insurance financed by general tax revenues, payroll taxes from employers and employees, and premiums paid by beneficiaries. It works on the principles of insurance. Premiums are paid by everyone to support the relatively few who become ill and need services. Not everyone, of course, will need services. Twenty percent of all beneficiaries account for 90 percent of the program's cost.[25] But when people do get sick, Medicare stands ready to pay for their care.

If Myers and other reporters had made accurate and more illuminating presentations of how Medicare actually worked, that would have helped people understand a program that has long baffled even the savviest beneficiaries.

The Media Research Center wasn't the only cop policing

journalists' vocabulary. Haley Barbour, then Republican National Chairman, vowed to raise "unshirted hell" with the news media whenever they used the word "cut." Barbour called network-news anchormen and correspondents, and held breakfasts and lunches with reporters, "educating" them on the difference between cuts and slowing Medicare's growth. Budget-committee chairman John Kasich phoned reporters warning them to avoid using the word "cut." Said Kasich: "I worked them over."[26]

The policework paid off. In September, *MediaNomics* reported "there has been a dramatic improvement in network labeling. Now half the time network reporters get it right labeling Medicare reform plans."[27] The National Journal reported that the *Los Angeles Times* stopped referring to "cuts" and started calling them "reductions in future growth in spending."[28]

When Republicans passed their bill on October 19, CBS carried the story on *The Evening News*. Linda Douglass, who had been criticized all summer by *MediaNomics,* got the words right. She told viewers that the Republican bill would double monthly premiums, create incentives to use managed care, and limit doctor and hospital fees, "all adding up to a savings of $270 billion in the growth of Medicare spending."[29] Douglass stressed the word "savings," avoided the word "cut," and gave a positive spin to a piece of legislation that was hardly in the interests of most Medicare beneficiaries. That still wasn't good enough for *Media Watch,* which noted, "Reporters spent October aiding liberal efforts to turn people against the GOP plan to balance the budget." It singled out Douglass, saying she "insisted on the October 20 *CBS Evening News* that the

President 'promised to veto the Republican plan to cut Medicare.'"[30]

A few days later on the *Today Show,* NBC Washington analysts Tim Russert and Lisa Myers struggled to get their lines straight. Russert said to *Today Show* co-anchor Katie Couric: "And in the end, Katie, the outline, the principles of slowing the great—rote, great of [*sic*]—growth rate of Medicare, welfare reform, tax cuts will be put in place." Myers, who was reporting on passage of the bill, stammered: "In most cases, the . . . the spending is—the growth of spending is being slowed . . ." Neither used the word "cut."[31]

Heritage Presses On

For the most part, Heritage avoided the war of semantics and pushed its voucher plan with the media and Congress. Its public-relations activities from summer on were continuous, well timed, and notable for their sheer volume, and illustrated how finely honed the technique of repetition had become. Heritage public-relations director Cheryl Rubin described their communications efforts: "We are always there. Members of Congress and their staffs see us out there in a timely fashion."[32]

Throughout the summer and into fall, Heritage was ever-present. At the end of June, the think tank sent out a news release titled "Heritage Foundation Recommends Major Medicare Reform," which quoted Stuart Butler. "The structural problems causing skyrocketing Medicare costs would be solved, and senior citizens would wind up with more health-care choices than they have now," Butler said. The release advocated switching from the current defined-benefit system to a defined contribution system similar to the Federal Employees Health Benefits Program.[33] For those who wanted to drill deeper, the release was accompanied by the twenty-two-page backgrounder "What to do about Medicare."[34]

The news media began to run with the Heritage story. The *Wall Street Journal* carried a small item in the back of the paper[35]; the *Washington Times* ran it in the A section with a lead that said: "The Heritage Foundation provided a glimpse of the kinds of reforms Republicans are considering in Medicare to avert bankruptcy and achieve $270 billion of savings by 2002."[36] Others in the media, particularly editorial writers, began promoting Heritage's ideas. The *Rocky Mountain News* embraced a defined-contribution plan: "The GOP concept has passed a 'field test'. The Federal Employees Health Benefits Plan [*sic*], which covers 9 million federal workers and their relatives, allows clients to browse a smorgasbord of insurance options . . . Congress should pass 'Medichoice'."[37] The *Commercial Appeal* in Memphis published a similar editorial, even using the same words.[38] Conservative columnist Cal Thomas relayed the Heritage message to his readers and challenged Republicans: "The Republican Congress must not shrink from true reform of a system that is headed for destruction no matter how much the Democrats lie about Medicare past, present, and future."[39]

By August, Heritage was firing a barrage of messages cleverly packaged in different ways to attract attention and offer the media new twists on the FEHBP plan. Rubin explained the strategy: "We laid down the foundation. When the debate goes on, you keep coming at it one way or another."[40]

And into the fall of 1995, as Congress moved closer to a vote on Medicare reform, Heritage came at the issue in several ways. A list of press releases shows the extent to which it tried to influence the media as the debate moved to a climax:

- August 8: A "Dear Journalist" letter from senior writer Mark Trapscott. The packet contained two papers, both F.Y.I.s: "A Guide to Medicare Reform Proposals," by policy analyst John Liu, which provided summaries of a number of reforms, and one by Stuart Butler, attacking the White House for using a different baseline than the Congressional Budget Office when discussing Medicare budget numbers.[41]
- September 19: An F.Y.I. called "What Americans Will Pay If Congress Fails to Reform Medicare: The State and Congressional District Impact."[42]
- September 22: An Executive Memorandum stamped RUSH in big red letters. The headline read: "Two Cheers for the House Medicare Plan."[43]
- September 25: A news release, "Federal Health Program Success Is Lesson for Medicare Reformers, Analyst Says," and a paper by Robert Moffit (the deputy director of policy studies), which discussed how the FEHBP program controls costs.[44]
- September 28: A "Dear Journalist" letter from Heritage public-relations associate Wanda Moebius. The letter high-lighted a factoid perhaps destined for radio talk shows: Medicare is "governed by 1,050 pages in the U.S. Code, 1,156 pages in the Code of Federal Regulations and guide-lines in the form of 19,150 pages in HCFA manuals and another 1,000 pages of HCFA 'rulings.'" Those facts, the press release noted, were found in the "Taxpayers Guide to

the Medicare Crisis," a blue and yellow Talking Points paper, which Heritage sent along with the letter.[45]

- October 6: A "Dear Editor" letter from Sam Walker, manager of editorial services. With it came a blue-bannered backgrounder, a paper written by a member of the Heritage Foundation Physicians' Council detailing what Heritage considered governmental red tape faced by clinical labs, and making a case for eliminating federal regulations governing them.[46]

- October 12: A "Dear Journalist" letter from Sam Walker accompanied by two op-ed essays. One, by Rep. Dan Miller, the Republican point man on Medicare, talked of a Medicare "miracle"—and the success in "making miraculous progress explaining what we are trying to do and why." Miller noted that journalists were beginning to get it right.[47] The second point-of-view paper, by Heritage health-care analyst Grace Marie Arnett, told people "What's Really at Stake in the Medicare Debate." The letter foreshadowed the content of Arnett's essay and got right to the nub of Heritage's campaign: "If Congress uses market-oriented strategies to restructure Medicare—and doesn't just raise taxes to cover rising costs—the 'bigger battle' over whether government or the private sector is going to solve our problems 'will practically be won.' "[48]

- October 16: A news release and an F.Y.I. discussing a computer study showing what businesses, employees, and consumers would have to pay if the Medicare payroll tax increased 3.52 percent to make up for the shortfall in the Hospital Trust Fund.[49]

- October 31: A news release and another backgrounder, this one by a clinical professor at Emory University who urged Congress to "apply key lessons from the private sector for reforming the Medicare system, especially by examining the remarkable degree of innovation in corporate plans that emphasize choice and competition."[50]

• November 14: A "Dear Journalist" letter along with an issue bulletin called "Reforming Medicare: Comparing the House and Senate Legislation." Policy analyst John Liu warned that failure to enact significant reform could mean "huge future tax increases on working families or deep cuts in benefits for the elderly."[51]

• November 16: A "Dear Journalist" letter accompanied by another F.Y.I. by John Liu to "set the record straight." The letter told journalists that the "too drastic" cuts in Medicare cited by Clinton in his veto message weren't cuts at all.[52]

• November 21: The F.Y.I. "Bridging the Budget Gap on Medicare," by Stuart Butler, resurrected the esoteric topic of baselines to measure ways of balancing the budget.[53]

Throughout late summer and into the fall, the ideas advanced in the Heritage papers and studies made their way into the media from different directions. Ohio congressman Martin Hoke wrote an op-ed in the *Cleveland Plain Dealer* using data from Heritage to show that without reform, average households in northeastern Ohio would have to pay on an extra 1,200 dollars a year in payroll taxes.[54] Butler wrote a 1,600-word essay for *Newsday* promoting the voucher plan.[55] He got an op-ed placed in the *Dayton Daily News*.[56] On the *MacNeil/Lehrer NewsHour* in October, Representative Dan Miller got another chance to promote Medicare choices.[57]

Congress passed the Medicare Preservation Act, which cut $270 billion from the program and laid the foundation for removing the federal government from the Medicare business. But the act was part of the larger budget bill that Clinton later vetoed. After the government shut down as a result of Clinton's veto, Congress passed a less drastic budget, and Medicare reform died. Nevertheless, Heritage had prepared Congress and the media for changes to come.

An Ineffective Counter-Campaign

During 1995, various interest groups tried to place other viewpoints on the public table, but these efforts were largely ineffective, partly because the media didn't want to listen and partly because the groups didn't have money to pursue an effective counterattack. Reporters either ignored them, or gave their ideas short shrift, usually in the form of a quote or two at the end of their stories.

"There was little effort among the media to examine the premises, arguments, assumptions, and claims" the Republicans were making, recalled Ed Rothschild, who directed communications activities for the grassroots group Citizen Action, which tried to buck the Heritage propaganda machine. (Citizen Action has since gone out of the Washington lobbying business.) "The definitions of the issues," said Rothschild, "were framed by the Republican leadership. The Republicans got away with wrapping themselves in the mantle of saving the program financially when they were dismantling its fundamental concepts."[58]

The media didn't report on the Luntz memo, which was an open secret among the press. In late July, nearly two months after the memo first surfaced, the *Washington Post* published a small story. The lead said that senior citizens'

135

groups were outraged by what they called a "condescending memorandum about Medicare." The story, which did not go into any particular depth or detail, was laced with quotes from Democratic politicians along with a particularly cogent statement from James Firman, president of the National Council on Aging. The memo, Firman said, "makes clear that their intent is to manipulate people's opinions. This isn't about solvency. It's about transferring income."[59] That notion got little attention in the media.

In late October, the *Post* published a more revealing story. It discussed the Luntz memo, other pollsters, and the tactics used by Congressional Republicans. It didn't, however, mention the Heritage Foundation or its media campaign.[60] By this time, Republicans had subsumed Heritage messages and solutions and integrated them into their own agenda.

As informative as the *Post* story was, it could not stop the Heritage steamroller. No single story, even one published by a respected national newspaper, can neutralize an effective public relations campaign, especially one that has been in place for years and is predicated on sheer repetition. "Fundamental change doesn't happen overnight. Plans must be carefully drawn up in advance and thought out with care," Heritage president Edwin Fuelner wrote in the think tank's newsletter that fall.[61]

Another grassroots group, Neighbor to Neighbor, using a small grant of $25,000 from an individual donor, conducted a counter-campaign of sorts, but it was too little too late. The group assembled a three-person team that included Ted Marmour, a health economist from Yale; Cathy Hurwit, then a health-care lobbyist with Citizen Action; and Edie Rasell, a physician and an economist with the Economic Policy Institute. It arranged for the team to meet network TV producers, reporters, and columnists. The group also distributed press packets that contained data aimed at exploding some of the Medicare "myths" the Republicans were using.

They succeeded in getting a few reporters to write clearer stories, but most of the press was still not interested in explaining what was really behind the Republican rhetoric about saving Medicare. The team made a few TV appearances, but couldn't stop Republican efforts or galvanize public opinion against the proposed reforms. Shelly Moskowitz, who directed Neighbor to Neighbor's Washington office, summed up the group's efforts: "Lobbying the media is just like lobbying the Congress. We need a lot more time and a lot more money. We can't even begin to compete."[62]

Ready to Fight Again

During 1996, Heritage issued a few releases about Medicare, but there was no serious discussion of reforming the program in an election year. At the beginning of 1997, Heritage revealed its new strategy in "Mandate for Leadership IV—Turning Ideas into Actions." In a brief postmortem on its 1995 activities, the document noted that the "education campaign" was "far from well crafted." It pointed out that "despite its limitations, however, it achieved a remarkable degree of success. Today there is much more interest in market-based reforms. The reason: Although the 1995 Medicare reform package ultimately fell to a Clinton veto, it demonstrated that an education campaign can change public attitudes regarding reform."[63] The 1997 document called for a new campaign "to prepare public opinion for Medicare reform." Such a campaign had to:

- convince Americans that Medicare provides inferior medicine and poor financial security
- convince Americans that Medicare cannot be sustained for long
- compare a reformed Medicare system to the Federal Employees Health Benefits Program
- protect current beneficiaries
- focus on "health care security"
- attract provider constituencies to support reform
- build bipartisan support first, then reinforce it with a commission[64]

In 1997, Heritage achieved most of its objectives. Building bipartisanship consensus was a snap, thanks to the groundwork laid two years earlier. The Mandate for Leadership concluded: "The untold story of the 1995–1996 debate on the issue is that while there was a heated debate about the amount of savings that should be sought in Medicare to stabilize the program's finances, there also were the makings of a consensus on the deeper structural reforms needed."[65]

Indeed, media accounts often described bipartisan efforts. In a story published in early June about a vote in the House Ways and Means Committee to make "sweeping changes in Medicare," Robert Pear of the *New York Times* wrote: "The bipartisan, cordial spirit of today's session was radically different from the strident, angry tone that characterized debates on Medicare in 1995 and 1996 when Democrats accused Republicans of trying to destroy the program."[66] Another Pear story published a few days earlier noted that Representative Pete Stark, a California Democrat, thanked Mr. Thomas (Representative Bill Thomas, the California Republican) for "his bipartisan efforts."[67]

Heritage got its Bipartisan Commission, which was no friend of social insurance. Half of the seventeen members accepted their appointments on the condition that they would not consider increasing revenues for the program. Most Medicare experts believe that if the program does not have more money, many elderly Americans may not receive medical care. But the commission gave little consideration to raising more revenue.

The 1997 media strategy was similar to the one Heritage used in 1995: Blitz the press with news releases, backgrounders, and F.Y.I.s to convince the media that Heritage's preferred solution—an FEHBP model for Medicare—was the only one. In February, Heritage issued a news release quoting deputy director of domestic policy studies Robert Moffit as saying the president's budget proposals for Medicare "do not represent a serious response" to structural problems with the program. It sent along a Heritage Talking Points paper to supplement the press release.[68]

Between February and August, when Congress passed the Balanced Budget Act, Heritage again came at the debate from several directions, never missing a chance to push the FEHBP model:

- March 31:   A "Dear Journalist" letter from Randy Clerihue, deputy director of editorial and media services. The letter noted that Heritage had just published a new study showing Congress how to balance the federal budget. The

139

mailing included the Heritage Foundation proposals for Medicare.[69]

- April 30: A backgrounder saying that time was running out for Medicare reform.[70]
- May 6: A news release quoting Stuart Butler, who said that budget cuts alone won't save Medicare.[71]
- May 9: A news release commenting on the budget deal between the president and Congress noting that a few key changes, including Medicare reform, would "dramatically" improve the budget agreement.[72]
- May 12: A "Dear Journalist" letter noting that the budget deal adds additional Medicare benefits, which Heritage called "an incredibly irresponsible idea." The letter also pushed the FEHBP model. The mailing included a backgrounder, by health-care policy analyst Carrie Gavora, arguing how the budget deal would increase Medicare benefit inflation. On the same day, Heritage issued another backgrounder, "The 1997 Budget Agreement: The Return of Big Government."[73]
- June 5: A "Dear Journalist" letter from Sam Walker, director of editorial services, that included Senate testimony by Stuart Butler pushing the FEHBP model.[74]
- June 12: A "Dear Journalist" letter from Randy Clerihue that included three papers, all of them promoting the FEHBP plan in some way. One was an issue bulletin that said the House plan did not give seniors health-care choices enjoyed by members of Congress, one was a backgrounder describing proposed legislation, and the third was an executive memorandum, stamped RUSH in big red letters, that discussed how the Medicare system could be reshaped.[75]
- June 16: A "Dear Journalist" letter, written by public-

relations associate Andrew B. Campbell. The letter included a backgrounder on the rise and repeal of the state of Washington's health-care plan, and advised journalists that Washington was now trying to use consumer choice and market competition to control health-care costs along the lines considered by Congress for Medicare.[76]

- June 27: A "Dear Journalist" letter telling the media that there was "light at the end of the seemingly endless, ever-darkening tunnel of Medicare reform."[77] Heritage sent along a story that had appeared in *The Economist* touting the Heritage Foundation proposal. (Recycling other media stories helps create a bandwagon effect.)[78]

- July 11: A "Dear Journalist" letter from Sam Walker. This offered help to reporters who might be having trouble sorting out the various Medicare reform proposals on the table. Help came in the form of an issue bulletin written by policy analyst Carrie Gavora. The bulletin, "How to Reform Medicare: A Reconciliation Checklist," described differences in various bills and promoted Heritage's position on a number of points.[79] The analysis also noted what Congress should do to reconcile the House and Senate versions of the legislation.

- August 5: A "Dear Journalist" letter from director of public relations Cheryl Rubin that included editorials from, as Heritage put it, "opinion leaders on both the left and the right (and in between)."[80] The mailing included editorials from *The Economist,* the *Cincinnati Post, Rocky Mountain News,* the *New York Times,* and the *Orange County Register,* which supported the Heritage plan. The latter quoted from a Heritage backgrounder sent to the media in June.[81] Heritage was making the most of recycling.

141

Partners for Change

The "Mandate for Leadership" outlined another strategy: target provider constituencies that could benefit from the reforms.[82] Allies who saw themselves benefiting from the various choice options that Heritage advanced became a potent lobbying force for change, reinforcing the objective of attracting support from providers.

The American Medical Association, never a fan of Medicare because the government controlled how much doctors could make from Medicare patients, furthered the notion of choice by supporting an option that allowed physicians to opt out of the system and contract privately with patients and charging them whatever the traffic would bear. The AMA also supported medical savings accounts, a free-market health-insurance solution successfully advanced in 1996 by another right-wing think tank, the National Center for Policy Analysis. (Medical savings accounts are one of the choices Heritage envisioned for its FEHBP model.)

The American Hospital Association pushed for provider-sponsored organizations, a form of managed care that allows the government to make capitation payments to hospital and doctor groups, which would then manage the care.

The National Right to Life organization promoted the private fee-for-service option, an arrangement in which insurance companies receive capitation payments, offer Medicare benefits (and perhaps extra coverage), and charge beneficiaries whatever they wish. If, over time, payments are too low to cover the rising costs of medical care, under this system beneficiaries would have to pay a greater share of the cost. Worried about rationing by managed-care companies, the right-to-lifers believed this option would let people buy their own coverage and avoid controls imposed by HMOs. They sent letters to every member of Congress threatening to support opposing candidates in the next election if members refused to include the private fee-for-service option in the legislation.

Even the AARP became an ally of sorts. AARP liked managed-care options for Medicare beneficiaries because they offered coverage for prescription drugs—a deficiency in the current program. According to the Mandate for Leadership, "potential opposition of some elderly organizations was defused [in 1995] because the plan gave these organizations an opportunity to profit by marketing their own plans to the elderly."[83] At a meeting on Medicare reform convened by the National Academy of Social Insurance (Stuart Butler was a co-chair), AARP chief lobbyist John Rother said: "The public may be more prepared than one might think for small steps that move Medicare in the direction of offering more choice and greater individual responsibility."[84]

A special ally was the United Seniors Association (USA), a conservative organization that boasts 600,000 members and bills itself as "the right voice for senior Americans." The group, formed as an offshoot of Republican operative Richard Viguerie's direct-mail fund-raising activities, still collects money through the mail. USA helped give cover to conservative efforts to cut Medicare while trying to weaken traditional organizations that represent seniors. It advanced its own proposal for reforming Medicare that included medical savings accounts, delaying the retirement age, giving seniors control over their Medicare funds, and offering a range of private options. In an issue analysis sent to members of Congress in 1996, United Seniors boasted that there were only three comprehensive reform proposals on the table—one from the AMA, one from Heritage, and theirs.[85]

It was after the Balanced Budget Act passed that United Seniors reached the peak of its influence. One of the options in the BBA allowed doctors to opt out of Medicare and contract privately with beneficiaries, an unwise course for most people since there are few protections against billing abuses. Doctors must agree to stay out of the program for at least two years, and patients cannot receive Medicare benefits for the services of that doctor while he or she is out of the program—a rule intended to prevent price gouging.

But the rule was too onerous for the AMA and Congressional conservatives. In late 1997, Representative Jon Kyl, an Arizona Republican, introduced legislation that would let doctors move into and out of Medicare whenever they wished, charge patients whatever they could get, and circumvent Medicare's billing protections.

United Seniors sprang into action, launching a direct-mail campaign to 1.4 million seniors asking for ten-, fifteen-, and twenty-five-dollar contributions to help repeal the ban. The mailing also included a petition for them to sign, demanding repeal. The solicitation letter was full of scary statements and erroneous information such as: "If Medicare denies you treatment, you will not be able to pay your Medicare doctor for care with your own money."[86] Medicare beneficiaries have always been able to pay for care that Medicare didn't cover.

United Seniors got press attention and gave prominence to what was essentially a non-issue, but one that had political value, in promoting the Kyl amendment. The group filed a lawsuit to overturn the two-year ban. The case has since been thrown out of court, but not before the group appeared on CNN and generated headlines such as these: "New Medicare Provision Causes Backlash among Seniors"; "Group Sues U.S. on Controversial Medicare Rule"; "Law makes it nearly impossible for seniors to get treatment outside of Medicare, even if they pay"; and this erroneous one in *USA Today,* "Elderly Call Medicare Rule Unfair—Freedom for seniors to pay for visits to the doctors of their choice, not allowed under Medicare rules, raises concerns of gouging, fairness."[87]

Media interest in the Kyl amendment continued into the spring of 1998. The Medicare Rights Center, a New York City advocacy group that counsels beneficiaries and distributes educational information, succeeded to some extent in refuting United Seniors' allegations. But often, remarks from the Center's director were inserted far down in a story. The Center found itself in a position similar to those of Citizen Action and Neighbor to Neighbor in 1995.

The Kyl amendment did not pass in 1998. Heritage weighed in on the issue, but it wasn't the major thrust of its health-care marketing efforts. In August, Heritage sent out a "Dear Journalist" letter along with a lengthy backgrounder on "How Congress Can Restore the Freedom of Senior Citizens to Make Private Agreements with Their Doctors."[88] The mailing also included a shorter version called "A Backgrounder—Executive Summary." Most of the year's public-relations activities focused on other issues.

The Kyl amendment was unfinished business for Heritage. But the larger issue of the public's business remains unfinished as well. The media's failure during the last round of legislative debate to explain the issues looming in Medicare and their negligence in providing context to their reports and failing to allow other voices into the discussion have created an electorate with a low level of knowledge about future options. The public is unprepared to support major changes that may be necessary or make choices that must be made. The public is not engaged in the debate.

In the fall of 1998, a survey by the Kaiser Family Foundation and the Harvard School of Public Health found that most Americans know little or nothing about the options being considered to change Medicare. Even among seniors, relatively few consider themselves well informed. Only 24 percent told Kaiser researchers that they had seen, heard, or read anything about Medicare Plus Choice, the name given to the program passed by Congress.[89] The Heritage Foundation was able to reshape Medicare, but three-quarters of the people immediately affected by the changes didn't know what they were.

Aftermath

In early 1999, the *New York Times* published the editorial "Making the Budget Bearable." It stated that "if Mr. Clinton's fiscal record is measured largely on the basis of what he does on Medicare, he risks a failing grade. He has proposed no long-term solution, rejecting an emerging consensus for turning Medicare into a competitive system like the one that provides a choice of health plans for every Federal employee."[90] The *Times'* editorial represented a near-triumph for The Heritage Foundation. The nation's premier newspaper had acknowledged that a consensus was building for an FEHBP-style of Medicare, and implied that this model might well be the appropriate solution.

When it looked like the Bipartisan Commission that Heritage proposed in its "Mandate for Leadership IV" might recommend the FEHBP plan, the think tank didn't miss the chance to take the credit. In a "Dear Journalist" letter dated January 26, 1999, Heritage crowed, "sometimes good ideas take years to germinate. Take Medicare. The Heritage Foundation first proposed in 1995 that the health-care system for America's elderly be reshaped along the lines of the Federal Employee Health Benefits Program (FEHBP)." In case journalists missed it the first time around, Heritage sent along an F.Y.I. from 1995 touting how well the FEHBP model controls costs, and a backgrounder on the FEHBP program written in 1992. The letter said Heritage experts Robert Moffit and Stuart Butler literally "wrote the book" on using the FEHBP model, and told reporters that both were available for interviews.[91]

Heritage has not quite reached its objective. The Bipartisan Commission dissolved in March 1999 without approving a proposal for reform. The commission could not reach agreement on a voucher plan put forward by commission chairman Senator John Breaux, a Democrat from Louisiana. Breaux's proposal would have transformed Medicare from a defined-benefit plan into a "premium support" plan. The term "voucher" had been replaced with the friendlier-sounding "premium support." The Breaux plan failed on a vote of 10–7, with all of the president's appointees voting against it.[92]

The voucher, alias premium-support plan, is far from dead.

In the spring of 1999, Breaux introduced legislation to reform Medicare along the lines advocated by Heritage, and there is support on Capitol Hill for such changes. In 1999 came reports that Medicare's spending had slowed dramatically for the first time in the program's history. The favorable financial news may slow down the momentum for a voucher plan. But if Heritage's past record is a guide, it may be just a matter of time until Medicare no longer resembles the social-insurance plan signed into law in 1965.

Conclusion: The Right Wing's Success

"To those who play or observe the Washington game, on both left and right, the influence of conservative think tanks is inescapable. Most impressive is the way in which conservative policy entrepreneurs have successfully won support for their grand story of American politics. If national politics can be seen largely as a contest of broad frameworks, there is little question that conservatives have won this game in recent years."[1]

— "$1 Billion for Ideas: Conservative Think Tanks in the 1990s"

The National Committee for Responsive Philanthropy

Right-wing think tanks have given a new meaning to ideological advocacy. They have redefined the role of scholarly institutions at both the federal and state levels whose mission was once to gently advise government officials with well-documented studies and research. Moving far beyond mere research, right-wing groups have turned themselves into roaring publicity machines with direct links to public policy and idea formation. They have built for themselves a measure of influence that surpasses that of the old-line think tanks and just about every other advocacy group around.

149

The "new ideas" advanced by the right are really just one idea dressed up in different clothes for different audiences. The central message they preach is simply laissez-faire economics—unfettered markets that allow business to pursue its quest for profits without the shackles of government interference while at the same time making the less fortunate fend for themselves. Whether the issue is welfare reform, tax cuts, privatizing Social Security, cutting programs for the poor, vouchers for Medicare beneficiaries, or less regulation of just about every economic enterprise, the underlying goal is the same.

To further that goal, right-wing think tanks have used inventive and clever media strategies to reach information elites as well as average citizens. They have successfully transformed their agenda into policy prescriptions that look intriguing even to good reporters.

In a flash, they can turn an obscure policy point into a press release that finds its way into the mainstream media or into the right-wing press. During health reform, for example, the Office of Management and Budget leaked some numbers about the cost of the Clinton health-care plan to officials at The Heritage Foundation. Heritage was able to quickly plant the numbers in a *Wall Street Journal* editorial, and they were in turn used by people on Capitol Hill. "There was a widespread assumption that there was something phony about the government claims," said Heritage senior fellow Dan Mitchell. "To some degree, it was an inside-the-Beltway story, but it was a nail in the health-plan coffin."[2]

Their campaigns also work far beyond the Beltway. A fiftyish man who lives in northern Wisconsin tells me with great conviction that he will never join the AARP. "Why?" I ask. He says the AARP has become too big and powerful and can get laws passed that benefit old people at the expense of children. The right's efforts to discredit the AARP have penetrated the consciousness of Americans far from Washington.

Right-wing think tanks have both created and exploited a vacuum of credible elites. By attacking academics and government bureaucrats, they have set themselves up as the only credible, independent sources of wisdom and information. These groups have been able to label themselves in a neutral way that somehow suggests they are the opposite of what they are. That aura of independence has worked its way into the media and rolled into public perception.

Why has the right been so successful at pushing its agenda via the media? There are, after all, other groups competing with their own studies, analyses, and reports that land on journalists' desks nearly every day. Why haven't the ideas and policy positions advanced by those organizations taken root and flowered in the press? The answers lie with journalists themselves, with the liberal or progressive organizations whose voices are barely a whisper, and, of course, with the public.

The Journalists

The current generation of journalists is now much more predisposed to accept the positions and conclusions advanced by the right on economic matters than were reporters of another era who had vivid memories of the Great Depression. That predisposition has been cultivated since the mid-1970s, first

151

by business lobbyist Charls Walker and later by others who argued that government spending and federal borrowing were bad because they crowded out private capital. By the mid-1970s, the business community had begun to talk in public forums about government spending and the federal debt. In the spring of 1977, for example, business and community leaders gathered at Columbia University's Arden House in upstate New York to hear about a relatively new idea—the need to generate more capital. Among the attendees at the university's American Assembly that year were mid-career journalists who were completing their year at Columbia on a Knight-Bagehot Fellowship, the goal of which was to prepare them to better report on business and finance. The reporters listened intently, and came away with a new perspective on covering economics.

By the mid-1980s, many journalists had come to accept the conservative orthodoxy that big government and government spending were evil because they sucked up money from individuals who could better use that money for themselves. In their role as truth seekers, journalists had embraced a new truth. The deficit became the only measure of whether or not public policy was working. Politicians who got the coverage were those brave enough to talk about cuts in cost-of-living adjustments and government programs that helped achieve the objectives of the "lower taxes–no deficit" ideology. People like Paul Tsongas "became heroes," recalls John Rother, AARP's chief lobbyist and a longtime Washington insider.[3]

Conventional wisdom holds that journalists are "liberal," but that widely accepted notion mixes up liberal leanings on social issues such as school prayer and abortion with a left-of-center bent on economic issues. It does not necessarily follow that reporters who are pro-choice or who voted for Bill Clinton are liberal on economic issues, or will cast their stories to favor progressive economic positions.

In 1980, a study by S. Robert Lichter, who heads the Center for Media and Public Affairs, one of the conservative media groups, found that journalists were "social progressives and lifestyle liberals"; they were largely pro-choice, seldom or never attended religious services, and endorsed strong affirmative-action measures for racial minorities. The study also noted that journalists had become more comfortable with the economic system than had their counterparts of an earlier era, and that 70 percent regarded the private-enterprise system as fair to workers. Only one in eight endorsed government ownership of big corporations.[4]

A study by the *Los Angeles Times* a few years later called newspaper journalists "super yuppies" who were "emphatically liberal on social issues and foreign affairs, distrustful of establishment institutions . . . and protective of their own economic interests."[5]

It's not surprising, then, that in 1998 FAIR, the liberal media watchdog group, discovered that on economic matters, such as taxes, corporate power, Medicare, Social Security, and trade, Washington journalists are more conservative than the general public. For example, 43 percent of the reporters thought too much power was concentrated in the hands of a few large companies, while 77 percent of the public did. Only 39 percent of the journalists saw a need to protect Medicare and Social Security against major cuts, compared to 59 percent of the public who felt that way.[6] Most journalists "would certainly not recognize themselves in the 'liberal media' picture painted by conservative critics," FAIR concluded.

FAIR's study also showed that most Washington journalists are financially well off, a happy circumstance that may make some of them less concerned about those who are not so fortunate. Half of the 444 journalists polled had household incomes exceeding $100,000, and nearly one-third had incomes greater than $150,000.[7] "Journalists are a pretty elite group," says James Warren, the Washington bureau chief of the *Chicago Tribune*. "They are more conservative than their image. . . . On welfare reforms they don't have ties to anyone who is particularly affected." When it comes to Medicare and Social Security, said Warren, "it's not like a lot of journalists are losing sleep over the issues. They don't understand or are not focusing [on them]." Warren added: "The right won the debate on stuff like welfare reform and free trade. A lot of journalists ended up agreeing with their basic assumptions."[8]

The predisposition of many journalists toward conservative solutions for economic problems sometimes makes them less prone to question reports from right-wing think tanks and look behind the numbers and logic their studies present. In 1995, the Times Mirror Center for The People & The Press surveyed journalists and found that about half of both local and national media respondents believed the press had not adequately covered the potential consequences of the Republicans' Contract with America. Even a majority of journalists who described themselves as conservative thought that the consequences of the Contract had been given too little coverage.[9]

Journalists may admit to pollsters that they have not always covered issues of economic importance to millions of Americans, but some haven't changed the way they report. In early 1998, The Heritage Foundation released a study claiming that Social Security was a bad deal for African Americans, particularly men.[10] Sixteen news outlets, including newspapers in major American cities, reported the Heritage findings, and many of those stories were presented in a way that supported Heritage's viewpoint.

The Heritage report, however, was later discredited by John Mueller, a Reagan Republican who works for a consulting firm headed by Lewis Lehrman, a name hardly associated with liberal causes. Mueller's study shows that African Americans actually lose under privatization[11] when transition costs, real-life earning patterns, and lower market projections are considered. The study was disseminated by the National Committee to Preserve Social Security and Medicare, a grassroots organization of some 5.5 million members that does not favor privatization. The Center on Budget and Policy Priorities also refuted Heritage with a study of its own, and officials of the Social Security Administration raised serious questions about the validity of the numbers Heritage used to make its case.

A Lexis-Nexis search shows that only three editorials mentioned Mueller's study, and only four news outlets reported the rebuttal by the Center on Budget and Policy Priorities that was presented at a press conference for Washington reporters. *U.S. Newswire* ran two stories, *Ethnic News Watch* ran one, and the *Los Angeles Times* carried a story based on the Center's report.

Heritage later rebutted its critics,[12] but a Nexis search

155

turned up no news organization that covered what it had to say. While supporters of the current system might have thought lack of coverage a good thing, the basic premise of the initial report remained in the public's mind and bolstered the idea that Social Security is a bad investment—the theme of so many media stories. The absence of any significant coverage of well-reasoned challenges to the report demonstrates how groups like Heritage command attention even when their facts are weak.

Did reporters avoid covering the challenges to the Heritage report knowing that their news organizations would not publish their stories, or did they report a story only to have it spiked? The answer may lie in the murky area of journalistic self-censorship.

In evaluating the right's success, one cannot discount the subtle and not-so-subtle signals from editors and publishers who discourage reporters from pursuing stories that hit too close to their own corporate interests, which often intersect with right-wing interests, particularly on economic matters.

As ownership of the media becomes concentrated in fewer hands, journalists may shy away from stories they know editors are loath to publish. A flap at ABC is a case in point. In the fall of 1998, ABC, which is owned by Disney, killed an investigation into the hiring practices at Disney's Magic Kingdom. The aborted story told of questionable practices that allowed convicted pedophiles to work at the resort. Shortly before ABC killed the story, Disney chairman Michael Eisner told National Public Radio, "I would prefer ABC not to cover Disney. . . . I think it's inappropriate for Disney to be covered by Disney. . . . By and large, the way you avoid conflict of interest, is to, as best you can, not cover yourself."[13] It's a safe bet that ABC reporters won't be suggesting stories about Disney any time soon.

If reporters don't decide on their own to avoid "inappropriate" topics, editors may dissuade them by suggesting that the stories being proposed are boring, are too complicated, or will take too long to do. Sometimes an editor may simply say that a story is just not good enough to run, or that the reporting is thin. If true, that's an acceptable reason; but if it's merely another way of warning a reporter to steer clear of forbidden territory, who is to know the difference? Eventually journalists get the message.

As *Mother Jones* publisher Jay Harris has written, every reporter knows what the "master narrative" is. They know they can fight so many battles and not any more. They know the rules, and that if they are broken too many times, they won't get ahead. "Reporters care more about fitting in to the master narrative than taking risks,"[14] Harris observed. He later told me that he defined master narrative, a term he borrowed from William Woo, the former editor of the *St. Louis Post-Dispatch,* as "the unwillingness of the corporate press and the commercial media to connect the dots between the facts of a given event and the overall economic implications for all of us."[15]

The Journalists' Rules

Journalistic convention has unwittingly helped advance the right wing's agenda. Take journalism's appetite for conflict and challenge to the status quo. Perhaps responding to the public's own cravings for conflict and challenge, the natural bias of any reporter is to look for confrontation and give prominence to news that challenges existing arrangements.

"The nature of the press is to use the words of people leading the argument," says CBS-TV correspondent Eric Engberg.[16] In recent years, those leading the argument have come from the right.

But too often the need for conflict and drama gets in the way of good reporting. "The most difficult thing to get the press to report on is the facts," says pollster Glen Totten, who heads Totten Communications, a firm that has worked for Democrats. "The entire coverage of shutting government [in 1995] was on who was winning and who was losing. Nobody focused on what was being discussed. The story was all about the game and politics, not about substance. When the entire press reports this way, it cheapens the discourse."[17]

The journalistic precepts of objectivity and balance also tend to work in the right's favor. In early 1999, at a meeting of Midwestern journalists who cover the aging beat, I, too, spoke about the importance of connecting the dots in report-ing—publicizing the consequences of actions advocated by various interest groups. What happens, for example, if rosy returns from the stock market don't materialize, or if women lose the protections built into the current Social Security sys-tem? Are we willing to accept the fact that more old people will be poor? If a voucher system for Medicare forces benefi-ciaries to assume a larger share of their health-care costs, will baby boomers want to pay for their parents' medical care when their parents can't pay for it themselves?

An older gentleman rose to take issue with my remarks. Journalists, he said, could not connect the dots because doing so edged too close to advocacy, which was best left for the editorial pages. Connecting the dots conflicted with balance, the man said, and he explained that reporters must give each side a quote, as if that was all there was to do.

Clearly, connecting the dots can be an ideologically laden act. Journalists can connect dots to confirm or conform to any conspiracy on the left or on the right. But connecting the dots goes beyond the promotion of either a left or a right point of view. It means making sure that there is a context and a factual connection to the dots; it requires making the last phone call to see if the facts tossed out to the public are indeed real, if the material disseminated by one group or another is more than innuendo or insinuation, if indeed reporters themselves are being used.

Discussing potential consequences of a proposal or idea and exposing different sides of the issue are not mutually exclusive. But doing both requires thinking beyond the "he said, she said" quotes; it calls for bolder presentations that move beyond the bland reporting that characterizes much of today's mainstream journalism. "The notion that if you get two sides you're telling the complete story is preposterous," says William Serrin, a professor of journalism at New York University. "The truth is more involved. We may be using objectivity as a shield or device that allows us not to be better reporters."[18] Counteracting right-wing spin and getting at the truth require a close look at the dots journalists may not want to connect.

Going beyond "he said, she said" quotes points out fundamental questions facing reporters today: Who really represents the public interest? Does any particular person or any particular group? Who can journalists really trust?

Because the right has been so successful at delegitimizing the academy and portraying organizations that were once accepted as representing the public as special interests, journalists

159

are at a loss for sources whom they believe can meet their tests of objectivity and neutrality. In the absence of what journalists perceive as a clear advocate for the public good, they tend to fall back on the "he said, she said" model and hope that somehow the public will understand what is at stake. Reporting boiled down to a pro and a con, however, often obscures whether the viewpoint represented reflects the interests of the public at large or the private advantages sought by a particular advocacy group on behalf of its members.

Balance without amplification keeps people in the dark. If amplification is given, it often favors the right simply because they are the challengers and have the money and the communications savvy to continually push their positions.

Furthermore, the whole idea of balance can be and has been manipulated. In recent years, all kinds of groups purporting to speak for the public have sprung up. Many are little more than front groups for other organizations or special interests, in the old-fashioned sense of the term. They have little standing or legitimacy to represent the public, and exist largely to provide the media with quotes from an opposing source. The right's United Seniors Association and 60 Plus were particularly effective during health reform and the Congressional debates on Medicare. Reporters often quoted them when they wanted a balance quote, or when Republican members of Congress wanted to present an alternative to the AARP. Reporters have little time and sometimes little inclination to find out who these groups are and what they represent.

The right always seems to be there. Whether it's because they have more money to further their agendas, or because they realize that the media is important, or simply because they are amply staffed with people who will deal courteously with the press, right-wing think tanks have a knack for knowing when reporters need angles to write about or a spokesperson to talk to. "They are interesting groups to talk to, especially on tax policy," explains one Washington reporter who often draws on conservative sources and declined to be named. What makes them so interesting? "Interesting ideas," he replies. This reporter says he doesn't try to give conservatives one quote and liberals another. Instead, he says, he gives more weight to groups "who supply me with information." What information? "Angles on these issues," he says.

A Weak Liberal Voice

Are the media entirely to blame for liberals' failure to communicate what they stand for? The answer clearly is "no." The same journalist who found conservative views interesting says that he doesn't know what the AARP is these days. "AARP is not a liberal group," he says. "They are mushy, mushy." The AARP can stand as a metaphor for other liberal organizations.

Many have acquiesced to the broad ideological assault that conservatives have launched against government and government programs. They have stood by and essentially failed to challenge the conservative view as being the appropriate approach for addressing social and economic issues. When they have mounted any opposition, many have not articulated their positions well. "Progressive groups tend to think in terms of technical arguments—policy wonkism—and don't think in terms of effective language and rhetoric," says Michael Pertschuk, co-director of the Advocacy Institute. "Most of these groups think of framing issues and rhetoric as being propaganda or public relations, which they associate with corporate interests. They think that's beneath them."[19]

Their ineffectiveness, however, is more than a matter of wonkish prose. Many progressive organizations seem almost afraid to articulate and stand for any position. Some, too, have begun to accept the deficit as the yardstick for evaluating public policy, and some, like the media, appear unwilling to connect the dots even when the connection might bolster their organizational objectives.

The right has succeeded in demonizing the premises of their opposition, and has scared opponents away from voicing what they stand for. Many liberals and progressive organizations are left to tinker at the margins with the proposals that the right puts forward.

"The rising strength of conservative policy institutions is likely to reinforce trends towards a greatly narrowed public-policy debate in the United States. At a time when national wealth and economic inequality are rising hand-in-hand, no real discussion is on the horizon for reviving the American ideal of shared prosperity," David Callahan wrote in his report for the National Committee for Responsive Philanthropy.[20]

Then there's the matter of money. Common wisdom has it that the right has more. But as Michael Shuman, who was a fellow at the Institute for Policy Studies, points out, foundations that support progressive causes actually have more money than conservative foundations, but too much of this money is spent foolishly. In a story appearing in *The Nation*, Shuman reported that assets of twelve key progressive foundations totaled nearly $8 billion in 1997. The assets of twelve key conservative foundations amounted to only $1.4 billion. Shuman gave several reasons why so-called progressive foundations are not as influential as those on the right: They fund narrowly defined issues; don't give general-support grants, which makes it harder to respond in the short run and to plan for the long run; give money for only one year; and, perhaps most important, they don't get involved in politics.[21]

Michael Pertschuk says that not long ago a representative of the Ford Foundation once told an Advocacy Institute official that "it would be a lot easier to fund you if the word 'advocacy' did not appear in your name." "It was a casual comment that illustrated an institutional frame of mind," Pertschuk recalled.[22] That is precisely the point. Mainstream foundations and the groups they fund don't see themselves carrying on an ideological battle. The foundations that fund conservative think tanks do.

Ask a liberal organization its position on Medicare or Social Security or how those programs should be funded, and you're apt to get a set of principles instead of concrete solutions. What reporter wants to write about principles? Many groups are not seriously pushing the issues they supposedly stand for. Although the number of uninsured is growing rapidly, and the patchwork solutions put in place to ameliorate the problem are ineffective, how many organizations are actively advocating for universal health insurance these days?

The right, on the other hand, continually pushes its issues even when they are not popular or seem far-fetched. Heritage has begun to market the idea of replacing employer-based health insurance with a system where people are on their own to buy any coverage they want—that is, if they can qualify for it. Such a system could evolve into a kind of health-insurance Darwinism, but if Heritage is ultimately successful in persuading Congress to turn Medicare into a voucher program, who knows what will happen to health insurance for those under sixty-five?

If progressive organizations are to reclaim ground in the ideological war, they must rethink what they stand for, be brave enough to tell the public, and sell their ideas more forcefully. Liberal groups need to persuade progressive foundations to give them money to do a better job of promoting their ideas. If more money is forthcoming, they must judiciously target their programs to change public perception. Big budgets don't always translate into effectiveness. The Capital Research Center was able to cripple the AARP with a budget significantly less than that of Ralph Nader's Public Citizen. Public Citizen, with a budget some three times larger, is hardly a significant player in national politics.

The Public's Stake

Both media organizations and the public have stakes in the information that is delivered. Media organizations faced with strong competition from many directions are under constant pressure to maintain readers, viewers, or listeners. Walker Lundy, the thoughtful editor of the St. Paul Pioneer Press, says that newspapers are paying far more attention to their audiences now because newspapers have so much more at risk than they once did.[23]

But are newspapers and other media outlets really producing what their audiences want? Pollster Glen Totten expresses one view: "The American public, for all the chest thumping, is ignorant at best and xenophobic at worst. They fundamentally don't care. We are participating less and less in the world."[24] When the public refuses to question a premise, such disengagement from politics helps right-wing organizations gain ground.

The public can hardly be expected to respond or to generate debate on issues unless those issues are framed in a meaningful way. People need to distinguish the important from the unimportant, the relevant from the irrelevant, the useful from the useless, and the truth from the falsehood, but they don't have an intrinsic judgment scale to do that job. If the media don't help, the public throws up its hands and withdraws.

How the media engages their audiences should be a question of more than academic interest. Has the public tuned out because the media have given them too little to latch on to, or too much? In a 1999 study, the Pew Research Center for The People & The Press found that media executives and journalists view the public as feeling overloaded by news and information. But Pew has also found that the public doesn't necessarily agree, since only 28 percent of the public say they are overloaded with information.[25]

The Pew findings point to a deep chasm dividing the media from the public. Have media executives and journalists misperceived their audiences, or are they simply rationalizing an unwillingness to provide information that the public may be thirsting to receive? Pew found that journalists also believe that declining numbers of readers, listeners, and viewers are due to their own lack of credibility with the public.[26] Does the credibility gap reflect the media's failure to provide the information the public seeks but is not receiving? "There's not much appetite among readers to say 'there's one more impossible problem,'" Walker Lundy says. "People don't like feeling overwhelmed and that they have no control. We're trying to point toward solutions."[27] Veteran journalist Gregg

165

Easterbrook put it this way: "Conservatives have made their arguments more interesting. Liberals argue problems while conservatives have very adroitly learned to argue solutions."[28]

Today the solutions that get the biggest play are coming from the right. Does the public's disconnection from the media indicate that they want to hear something else? If so, where will they turn to get it?

As we move into a new century, perhaps it is time to re-think what journalism should be about; to construct a new framework for informing the public. Technology now makes it possible for the public to inform itself, with all kinds of interests vying for their attention and no gatekeepers to get in the way, or—to take a more positive view—to guide them through the shoals of self-interest, bias, propaganda, misinfor-mation, and outright lies that lurk in hundreds of Web sites on the Internet.

The right's success in transforming the debate over the last twenty years shows how outmoded the old precepts of jour-nalism have become. As James Carey, professor of journalism at Columbia University, pointed out so eloquently a decade ago: "We have a journalism that reports the continuing stream of expert opinion, but because there is no agreement among experts, it is more like observing talk-show gossip and petty manipulation than bearing witness to the truth. We have a journalism of fact without regard to understanding through which the public is immobilized and demobilized and merely ratifies the judgments of experts delivered from on high. It is above all a journalism that justifies itself in the public's name but in which the public plays no role except as an audience: a receptable to be informed by experts and an excuse for the practice of publicity."[29] Carey's critique is even more relevant today.

The right wing's mastery of publicity, and its success in shutting out other points of view and turning major issues affecting millions of people into lopsided discourse, shows that this kind of journalism is just not good enough.

Notes

INTRODUCTION

1. Pierre Thomas, "One Out of Four Federal Prisoners Not a U.S. Citizen; Drug Trade Major Factor in Rising Detention Rate," *Washington Post,* 25 November 1994, p. A1.
2. "Helms and a Real Issue," Denver *Rocky Mountain News,* editorial, 25 November 1994, p. 71A.
3. Richard Wolf, "Congressional Leaders Still Campaigning; House, Senate Members Vie for Party Posts," *USA Today,* 25 November 1994, p. 4A.
4. "The Welfare Gap—Problem No. 1: The Children," Myron Magnet, *New York Times,* 25 November 1994, p. 37.
5. "$650 a Baby: Germany to Pay to Stem Decline in Births," Stephen Kinzer, *New York Times,* 25 November 1994, p. 3.
6. "Helping the Needy; Political Wrap," The *MacNeil/Lehrer NewsHour* (Educational Broadcasting and GWETA: 25 November 1994).
7. Dan Mitchell, senior fellow, The Heritage Foundation, interview with author.
8. Sidney Blumenthal, *The Rise of the Counter Establishment* (New York: Harper & Row, 1988), pp. 37, 43.
9. Jeanette Goodman, vice president, National Center for Policy Analysis, interview with author.

10. Sally Covington, "Moving a Public Policy Agenda: The Strategic Philanthropy of Conservative Foundations" (Washington, D.C.: National Committee for Responsive Philanthropy, July 1997), p. 23.
11. Sally Covington, op. cit., p. 5.
12. The Foundation Grants Index, 27th Edition, The Foundation Center, 1999, p. 1526.
13. David Callahan, *$1 Billion for Ideas: Conservative Think Tanks in the 1990s* (Washington, D.C.: National Committee for Responsive Philanthropy, March 1999), p. 7.
14. Jeanette Goodman, op. cit.
15. Lisa McGiffert, Consumers Union, interview with author.
16. Cheryl Rubin, interview with author.
17. Michael Pertschuk, interview with author.
18. "On the Media," WNYC, May 1994.
19. Krieble Institute, Free Congress Foundation, Satellite Conference "How to Manage the Media II," Washington, D.C., 27 January 1996.
20. Howard Kurtz, "The Bad News Starts at Work in the Nation's Newsrooms," *Washington Post,* 30 October 1995, p. A8.
21. Jeremy Iggers, "Get Me Rewrite," *Utne Reader* (September–October 1997), p. 46f.
22. Dane Smith, statehouse reporter, *Minneapolis Star Tribune,* interview with author.
23. Karen Rothmyer, "Citizen Scaife," *Columbia Journalism Review* (July–August 1981), p. 50.

CHAPTER 1.
THE RIGHT WING MEETS THE PRESS

1. Dan Mitchell, senior fellow, The Heritage Foundation, interview with author.
2. John W. Cooper, "Fifty Laboratories of Democracy: Changing

Public Policy in the States Will Change Everything," *The Madisonian Journal,* spring 1994, vol. 2, no. 1, p. 1.

3. Lawrence Mone, president, the Manhattan Institute, interview with author.

4. Confidential memorandum, "Attack of American Free Enterprise System," from Lewis F. Powell, Jr., to Eugene B. Snyder, Jr., chairman, Education Committee, U.S. Chamber of Commerce, 23 August 1971.

5. Charles E. Lindblom, *The Policy-Making Process* (Englewood Cliffs, NJ: Prentice-Hall, Inc., 1980), pp. 71–94.

6. Michael Pertschuk, co-director, The Advocacy Institute, interview with author.

7. "Endnotes," *CEI Update* (Competitive Enterprise Institute newsletter), vol. 8, no. 4, April 1995, p. 8.

8. Reese Cleghorn, "The Press Shifts to the Right, But Slowly," *American Journalism Review,* December 1994, p. 4.

9. *This Week with David Brinkley,* American Broadcasting Company, 20 October 1996, and *ABC World News Tonight,* 23 October 1996.

10. "Tax Report," *Wall Street Journal,* 30 October 1996, p. 1.

11. *This Week with David Brinkley,* op. cit.

12. Lawrence Mone, op. cit.

13. Ibid.

14. Memorandum from Lawrence Mone, president, Manhattan Institute, to supporters, March 1996.

15. John Stossel, "The Trouble with Lawyers," *20/20 ABC News Special* (New York: American Broadcasting Co., 2 January 1996), unpaginated transcript.

16. Ibid.

17. John Stossel, "Protect Us from Legal Vultures," *Wall Street Journal,* 2 January 1996, p. 8.

18. Memorandum from Lawrence Mone, president, Manhattan Institute, to friends and supporters, March 1998, p. 2, and

memorandum from Lawrence Mone, to friends and supporters, August 1998, p. 2.

19. John Stossel, speech at Manhattan Institute seminar, 20 January 1999.

20. Invitation letter from Lawrence Mone, president, Manhattan Institute, to attend seminar "Order in the Court: A Fresh Look at Legal Reform," 30 December 1998.

21. "There Are Watchdogs and There Are Watchdogs," *National Journal,* 30 November 1996, p. 2587.

22. Bonnie Goff, Media Research Center, interview with author.

23. Jim Naureckas, editor of *Extra,* interview with author.

24. Tim Graham, Media Research Center, interview with author.

25. *The Foundation Grants Index*, 1995, 23rd edition, The Foundation Center, p. 117, and *The Foundation Grant Index*, 1996, 24th edition, The Foundation Center, p. 63.

26. *The Foundation Grants Index*, 1997, 25th edition, The Foundation Center.

27. *The Foundation Grants Index*, 1998, 26th edition, The Foundation Center.

28. "Taxes and Savings," *MediaNomics,* January 1999, p. 2.

29. Tim Graham, op. cit.

30. "Kudos," *MediaNomics,* October 1998, p. 3.

31. "Kudos," *MediaNomics,* December 1998, p. 3.

32. "Kudos," *MediaNomics,* January 1999, p. 3.

33. Paul Starobin, "Heeding the Call," *National Journal,* 30 November 1996, p. 2584.

34. Howard Kurtz, "The GOP Finds an Ally in an Unexpected Paper," *The Washington Post,* 13 December 1995.

35. Carol Felsenthal, *Power Privilege and the Post: The Katherine Graham Story* (New York: G. P. Putnam's Sons, New York, 1993), p. 416f.

36. S. Robert Lichter, Daniel Amundson, and Linda S. Lichter,

Balance and Diversity in PBS Documentaries (Washington, D.C.: Center for Media and Public Affairs, March 1992), p. 159.

37. David Croteau and Williams Hoynes, *By Invitation Only: How the Media Limit Public Debate* (Monroe, Maine: Common Courage Press, 1994), p. 141f.

38. Ibid., pp. 141–43.

39. "PBS Watchdog," *Organization Trends* (Washington, D.C.: Capital Research Center, May 1995), p. 3.

40. *Buying a Movement: Right Wing Foundations and American Politics* (Washington, D.C.: People for the American Way, 1996), p. 12.

41. David Croteau and William Hoynes, op. cit., p. 141.

42. James Ledbetter, "Public Broadcasting Sells Out," *The Nation,* 1 December 1997, p. 12.

43. Trudy Lieberman, "Stacked Deck," *The Nation,* 21 July 1997, p. 10.

44. Ibid.

45. Alex Jones, interview with author.

46. Trudy Lieberman, op. cit., p. 10.

47. Philip Shenon, "Half of Gulf-Illness Panel Now Calls Gas a Possible Factor," *New York Times,* 19 August 1997, p. A15.

48. Philip Shenon, "Expert Panel Says Pentagon Ignored Evidence of Poison Gas," *New York Times,* 31 October 1997, p. A24.

49. "Agenda '97," *The NewsHour with Jim Lehrer,* 10 February 1997, PBS, Transcript #5761.

50. Jim Naureckas, editor of *Extra,* interview with author.

51. *CEI Update,* September 1998.

52. Michael Tanner, Cato Institute, interview with author.

53. Lawrence Mone, op. cit.

54. 1997 Annual Report (Washington, D.C.: Cato Institute, 1997), p. 44.

55. Tim Weiner, "A Congressman's Lament on the State of Democracy," *New York Times,* 4 October 1999, p. A14.

56. Dan Mitchell, op. cit.
57. "The State and District Impact of the Clinton Tax Increase," *Backgrounder* (Washington, D.C.: The Heritage Foundation), 7 April 1994.
58. "Notes for Taxday, 1996," Citizens for Tax Justice, 7 April 1996, p. 3f.
59. "Significant Tax Vote Over the Past Decade: A Congressional Tax Report Card," Citizens for Tax Justice, August 1966, p. 6.
60. James Ridgeway, "Heritage on the Hill: The Right's Pre-eminent P. R. Machine," *The Nation,* 22 December 1997, p. 16.
61. Rex Nelson, "Building a Conservative Juggernaut: First GOP-Led Congress in Decades Gives Think Tank Power to Shape Laws," *Arkansas Democrat Gazette,* 5 November 1995, p. 1A.
62. Charles Lindblom, op. cit., p. 82.
63. *The Heritage Foundation's 25th Anniversary Gala & Leadership for America Lecture,* 10 December 1997 (Washington, D.C.: The Heritage Foundation), p. 4.
64. Ibid., p. 19.
65. Brent Bozell, Media Research Center, interview with author.

CHAPTER 2.
WOUNDING THE ENEMY:
THE ATTACK ON AARP

1. *The Chronicle of Philanthropy,* 21 September 1995, p. 35.
2. "Whose Kingdom? The Blurring Lines Between Pat Robertson's Money and Politics," Michael Smith, *Sojourners Magazine,* November–December 1995.
3. Capital Research Center, untitled publicity brochure.
4. Thomas J. DiLorenzo, *Frightening America's Elderly: How the Age Lobby Holds Seniors Captive* (Washington, D.C.: Capital Research Center, 1996), chapter 2.

5. Ibid., p. 24.

6. Ibid., p. 23.

7. Capital Research Center, *Organization Trends,* 1994.

8. Ibid.

9. Plaque at Capital Research Center headquarters.

10. Capital Research Center, *Annual Report,* 1997.

11. "In the News," Capital Research Center, summer 1995.

12. Ibid.

13. Capital Research Center, untitled publicity brochure.

14. Capital Research Center, *Annual Report* (Washington, D.C., 1994).

15. Capital Research Center, *Annual Report* (Washington, D.C., 1997).

16. *Foundation Grants Index*, 1995, 23rd edition, The Foundation Center, p. 1221.

17. Capital Research Center, *Annual Report* (Washington, D.C., 1994), p. 12.

18. *Foundation Grants Index*, 1996, 24th edition, The Foundation Center, p. 1278.

19. *Foundation Grants Index*, op. cit., p. 1278.

20. Capital Research Center, Publication Catalogue (Washington, D.C., November 1998).

21. *Foundation Grants Index*, 1996, 24th edition, The Foundation Center, p. 1268.

22. Op. cit., p. 1285.

23. Ibid., p. 1313.

24. *Foundation Grants Index*, 1997, 25th edition, The Foundation Center, p. 1274.

25. *Foundation Grants Index*, 1999, 27th edition, The Foundation Center, p. 1471.

26. *Foundation Grants Index*, 1998, 26th edition, The Foundation Center, p. 1348.

27. "Capital Report," Capital Research Center newsletter (Washington, D.C., Winter 1995), p. 4.

28. Rich Lowry, "Grant Children," *National Review* (6 February 1995), pp. 21–22.

29. "Capital Report," Capital Research Center newsletter (Washington, D.C., winter 1995).

30. "Uncovered—the AARP: A Taxpayer-Financed 900-Pound Guerilla," Intellectual Ammunition, March/April 1995, p. 4.

31. Alan Simpson, "AARP and the Politics of Deception," *Washington Times* (16 February 1995, op-ed), p. A21.

32. Andrew Mollison, "Senator Zeroes in on AARP Finances," *Austin American-Statesman* (28 March 1995), p. A1.

33. Stephen Green, "Senate Probing AARP Tax Status," *San Diego Union-Tribune* (4 May 1995), p. A1.

34. Vic Ostrowidzki, "Senator Challenges Non-profit Status of Elderly Lobby," Albany, N.Y., *Times Union* (21 May 1995), main, p. E6.

35. Lance Gay, "AARP Seniors—First Agenda Paralyzes Deficit-Reduction Efforts," *Atlanta Journal-Constitution* (23 April 1995), perspective, p. 2C.

36. "Senator Lists Top 10 Gripes with the AARP," *St. Petersburg* (Florida) *Times* (16 July 1995), p. 3A.

37. Carolyn Lochhead, "Senator Takes on AARP," *San Francisco Chronicle* (4 May 1995), p. A1.

38. *This Week with David Brinkley*, American Broadcasting Company, 7 May 1995.

39. "The Big Barbecue," *Indianapolis Star* (20 June 1995), p. A4.

40. "Gorilla," *Cincinnati Enquirer* (18 June 1995), editorial, p. G2.

41. Philip Terzian, "Simpson Shows He Has Mettle to Take on Powerful AARP," *Arizona Republic* (27 June 1995), editorial/opinion section, p. B5.

42. "The Silver Network," *Providence Journal-Bulletin* (29 June 1995), editorial section, p. 8B.

43. Thomas W. Waldron, "Lobbyist or Entrepeneur? AARP Undergoes Scrutiny," *Baltimore Sun* (28 May 1995), p. 1A.

44. Linda Chavez, "Exposing AARP for What It Is," *Cincinnati Enquirer* (3 July 1995), editorial, p. A12.

45. "The Business of AARP," *Wall Street Journal* (25 May 1995), editorial.

46. *ABC World News Tonight*, American Broadcasting Companies, Inc. (13 June 1995).

47. Channel 29 News, WTXF—Fox Network (13 June 1995).

48. Lance Gray, op. cit.

49. "Finance Subcommittee to Hear Testimony on the American Association of Retired Persons (AARP)," U.S. Senate Committee on Finance (Washington, D.C., June 12, 1995). *See also* Thomas McArdle, "Golden Oldies: American Association of Retired Persons' Liberalism," *National Review,* Vol. 47, no. 17 (11 September 1995), p. 44.

50. "Frightening America's Elderly," op. cit., pp. 83, 85.

51. John Rother, interview with author.

52. "Sen. Simpson Blasts 'Hypocrisy' of AARP," (Memphis) *Commercial Appeal* (21 June 1995), p. 4A.

53. Joe Klein, "AARP? ARRGH," *Newsweek* (15 May 1995), p. 27.

54. John Hall, "Simpson Nearly the Lone Senator at AARP Hearings," *Sacramento Bee* (24 June 1995), p. B7.

55. Elizabeth Mehren and Robert A. Rosenblatt, "For AARP, a Reversal of Fortune," *Los Angeles Times* (22 August 1995).

56. Matt Miller, "Senator Alan Simpson Takes on the Powerful AARP," Morning Edition, National Public Radio (14 June 1995).

57. Trudy Lieberman, "GOP 'Mediscare,'" *The Nation* (6 November 1995), p. 539.

58. Ibid.

59. John Rother, interview with author.
60. "Can You Trust the AARP?" *New York Times,* 20 May 1996, p. A14.
61. "Kudos: AARP, Tax Code Come Under Fire," *MediaNomics* (Media Research Center, August 1997).
62. John Rother, interview with author.
63. Ibid.
64. Michael Tanner, Cato Institute, interview with author.
65. John Rother, op. cit., interview with author. *See also* Jeanne Cummings, "AARP, Usually Vocal, Opts for Neutral Stance in Politically Volatile Debate on Social Security," *Wall Street Journal* (2 December 1998), p. A24.
66. James L. Martin and Donald J. Senese, "Taxpayers Fund Lobby for 'Senior-Friendly' Government Pork, Programs and Perks," *Organization Trends* (Washington, D.C.: Capital Research Center, January 1998).
67. Op. cit.
68. Horace B. Deets, "Social Security Reform: We Should Make it Happen," *AARP Bulletin* (June 1999), p. 21.

CHAPTER 3.
REMOVING AN OBSTACLE:
"MODERNIZING" THE FDA

1. Competitive Enterprise Institute, *Annual Report* (Washington, D.C., 1994), p. 2f.
2. Lizette Alvarez, "By Large Margin, Senate Votes to Streamline F.D.A.," *New York Times* (25 September 1997), p. A20; Katharine Q. Seelye, "Major Overhaul for F.D.A. as President Signs New Law," *New York Times* (22 November 1997), p. A10.
3. Public Citizen, "Consumers Blast White House Signing Cer-

emony for Anti-FDA Bill," news release (20 November 1997).

4. U.S. Food and Drug Administration, "The Food and Drug Administration: An Overview" (http://www.fda.gov/opacom/hpview.html).

5. Public Citizen, press release, op. cit.

6. Thomas Moore, George Washington University, interview with author.

7. Peter Stone, "The Demolition Prescription: Industry Leaders and Lawmakers Want to Overhaul the Food and Drug Administration," *Orlando Sun-Sentinel* (26 March 1995), p. G1.

8. Thomas Moore, op. cit., interview with author.

9. Saul Friedman, "Medicine May Be Hard to Swallow," *Newsday* (23 February 1995), p. A41.

10. Saul Friedman, "Republicans Targeting FDA," *Newsday* (27 February 1995), p. A4.

11. Reginald Rhein, "Congress, Health Care Groups Push for Faster FDA," *Biotechnology Newswatch* (6 February 1995), p. 1.

12. *Americans on Deregulation,* A Special Report From Luntz Research (Arlington, Va: The Luntz Research Companies, n.d.), p. 7.

13. Ibid.

14. Ibid.

15. James Bovard, "Double-Crossing to Safety," *American Spectator*, Vol. 28, no. 1 (January 1995), p. 24.

16. James Bovard, "Medical Follies at the FDA," *Washington Times* (20 December 1994), p. A17.

17. Cato Institute Annual Report, 1994, p. 33; Competitive Enterprise Annual Report, 1994, p. 27.

18. Mona Charen, "Big Brother FDA," *Baltimore Sun* (3 January 1995), p. 11A.

19. Edwin Feulner, Jr., "Bringing Back the Reagan Agenda," *Washington Times* (10 January 1995), commentary, p. A17.

20. Craig E. Richardson and Geoff C. Ziebart, *Red Tape in America* (Washington, D.C.: The Heritage Foundation, 1995), p. 22f.

21. Anna Bryce, Amway spokesperson, interview with author.

22. *Annual Report*, The Heritage Foundation, 1997, p. 48.

23. Ibid.

24. "Soft Money in the 1993–1994 Election Cycle," Center for Responsive Politics (http://www.opensecrets.org/parties/soft93.htm).

25. "Top 50 Individual Contributors, 1993–1994 Election Cycle," Center for Responsive Politics (http://www.opensecrets.org/indivs/cgi-win/indivs.exe).

26. "Dietary Supplement Health and Education Act of 1994," Center for Food and Safety and Applied Nutrition, U.S. Food and Drug Administration (1 December 1995) http://vm.cfsan.giv/~dms/dietsupp.html.

27. Denise Grady, "Articles Question Safety of Dietary Supplements," *New York Times* (17 September 1998), p. A24.

28. "Our Story," Amway (http://www.amway.com/Our Story/o-prodNutril.asp).

29. Peter H. Stone, "Ganging Up on the FDA," *National Journal* (18 February 1995), p. 411.

30. Federal News Service, 31 January 1995, prepared testimony of C. Boyden Gray.

31. Peter H. Stone, op. cit., p. 412.

32. "Group Calls for FDA Reform, Says Delays Cost Lives, Money," *BNA Health Care Daily* (13 January 1995).

33. Saul Friedman, "Republicans Targeting FDA," op. cit., p. A4.

34. *Foundation Grants Index*, 1997, 25th edition, The Foundation Center, pp. 334, 1316.

35. *Foundation Grants Index*, op. cit., p. 343.

36. Ibid., p. 339, and *Foundation Grants Index*, 1996, 24th edition, The Foundation Center, p. 329.
37. Peter H. Stone, op. cit., p. 413.
38. Ibid.
39. Advertisement of the Washington Legal Foundation, "The Problem with Health Care in America is the FDA," as seen in the *Wall Street Journal* and *National Journal*.
40. "FDA 'Horror Story' Proves Unfounded," *New York Newsday* (25 February 1995), p. A13.
41. Letter to Daniel J. Popeo, chairman and general counsel, Washington Legal Foundation, from James A. O'Hara III, associate commissioner for public affairs, U.S. Department of Health & Human Services, 25 January 1995.
42. " 'So Safe You Could Die'—Overregulation by the FDA," *20/20*, American Broadcasting Company (12 August 1994).
43. "FDA 'Horror Story' Proves Unfounded," op. cit., p. 13.
44. Letter to Daniel J. Popeo, op. cit.
45. Michael Waldholz, "Genentech Inc. Pressed by Data on Clot Drugs," *Wall Street Journal* (27 March 1992), p. B3.
46. Letter to Daniel J. Popeo, op. cit.
47. Ibid.
48. Ibid.
49. Ibid.
50. Lauran Neergaard, "Critics Attack FDA," *Santa Cruz County Sentinel* (30 January 1995), p. A1.
51. "FDA 'Horror Story' Proves Unfounded," op. cit. "No, the FDA Is Not Killing People." *Consumer Reports,* Vol. 60, no. 4, April 1995, p. 218.
52. Philip J. Hilts, "F.D.A. Becomes Target of Empowered Groups," *New York Times* (12 February 1995), p. A24.
53. William G. Castagnoli, "What Is the WLF and Why Is It Challenging the FDA?" *Medical Marketing & Media* (CPS Communications, Inc: April 1995).

54. Sam Kazman, general counsel, Competitive Enterprise Institute, interview with author.

55. *Foundation Grants Index*, 1999, 27th edition, The Foundation Center, p. 1526.

56. Louis Jacobson, "Tanks on the Roll," *National Journal,* 8 July 1995, p. 1767.

57. Sam Kazman, op. cit., and "CEI Says Solve Drug Lag by Changing Agency Veto to Certification of Unapproved Products," *BNA Health Care Daily* (Washington, D.C.: The Bureau of National Affairs, Inc., 13 January 1995).

58. Sam Kazman, op. cit., and "The FDA in the New Washington," *Chicago Tribune* (4 February 1995), editorial section, p. 16.

59. Sam Kazman, "The FDA in the New Washington," op. cit.

60. Sam Kazman, op. cit., interview with author.

61. Competitive Enterprise Institute, "Institute Wines for Free Speech," press release (Washington, D.C.: 8 May 1995).

62. Sam Kazman, op. cit., interview with author.

63. "Public in Dark about Alcohol & Heart Disease," press release (Washington, D.C.: Competitive Enterprise Institute, 6 November 1995).

64. Jeff Jacoby, "Feds Slow to Wake up to Alcohol's Healthful Effects," *Boston Globe* (9 January 1996), op-ed section, p. 15.

65. David Stout, "Government Allows Labels About Wine's Benefit," *New York Times* (6 February 1999), p. 13.

66. Michael Massing, "Wine's Unfortunate New Labels," *New York Times* (9 February 1999), op-ed section, p. A23.

67. Sam Kazman, op. cit., interview with author.

68. Ibid., and letter to Dr. David Kessler, commissioner, U.S. Food and Drug Administration, from Sam Kazman, general counsel, Competitive Enterprise Institute, 25 October 1995.

69. Brigid Schulte, "Why Not Regulate Coffee, Too? Tobacco

Funded Think-Tank Asks," (Montreal) *Gazette* (25 October 1995), p. D13.

70. Competitive Enterprise Institute, "Cancer Specialists to FDA: 'Get Out of Our Way,'" press release (Washington, D.C.: 15 August 1995).

71. James Bovard, "Heavy FDA Hands on Therapy," *Washington Times* (30 September 1995), commentary, p. C1.

72. "FDA's Vendettas," *Washington Times* (8 October 1995), editorial, p. B2.

73. Donna Kelley, "Conservative Policy Analyst Urges Cancer Cuts," KCBS News (San Francisco: KCBS Radio News, 14 November 1995).

74. John Berlau, "Dr. Kessler, Remove the Gag," *Wall Street Journal* (5 December 1995), p. 20.

75. Doug Bandow, "The FDA May Cost You Your Life," *Washington Times* (18 December 1995), op-ed, p. A21.

76. Sam Kazman, op. cit., interview with author.

77. Edward Hudgins, Cato Institute, interview with author.

78. Robert Pear, "Lawyers and Lobbyists Help Guide Effort by Republicans to Speed Drug Approvals," *New York Times* (4 March 1996), p. A15.

79. *Cato Handbook for Congress* (Washington, D.C.: Cato Institute, 25 January 1995), p. 200f.

80. Robert Goldberg, "An FDA Smoke Screen," *Wall Street Journal* (15 August 1995), p. A16.

81. Edward Hudgins, op. cit.

82. *Nightline*, ABC News, American Broadcasting Companies, Inc. (18 March 1996).

83. Congress Watch, "A Million for Your Thoughts: The Industry-funded Campaign Against the FDA by Conservative Think Tanks," (Washington, D.C.: Public Citizen, 1996), pp. 1–12.

84. "Drug, Medical Device, Biotech and Tobacco Companies Gave at Least $3.5 Million for Deceptive Anti-FDA Campaign," news release (Washington, D.C.: Public Citizen, 24 July 1996).

85. "FDA: Drug, Tobacco Companies Funded Anti-Regulation Efforts," *Health Line* (American Political Network, Inc., 24 July 1996), and "Drugmakers Et Al Accused of Anti-FDA Campaigning," *Market Letter* (Information Access Company, a Thompson Corporation Company, 23 August 1996).

86. Maura Kealy, Public Citizen, interview with author.

87. "Cardiac and Cancer Specialists on the Need for FDA Reform," press release (Washington, D.C.: Competitive Enterprise Institute, 24 July 1996).

88. Sam Kazman, op. cit., interview with author.

89. Julie Defalco, "Advocacy, Politics and Reforming the FDA," *Washington Times* (15 August 1996), p. A19.

90. Maura Kealy, op. cit., interview with author.

91. George Strait and Peter Jennings, "Recalled Fen-Phen, Redux Worse than Thought," *World News Tonight with Peter Jennings,* transcript (New York: ABC News, 24 September 1997).

92. Frank Clemente, "A Pandora's Box of Drug Legislation," *New York Times,* 17 September 1997, p. 31.

93. "Safety Jitters," *Washington Post,* editorial (22 September 1997), p. A17.

94. "New CEI Study: Promising Treatments Delayed by FDA," press release (Washington, D.C.: Competitive Enterprise Institute, 26 February 1997).

95. Katharine Q. Seelye, "Major Overhaul for F.D.A. as President Signs New Law," *New York Times,* 22 November 1997, p. A10.

96. Saul Friedman, "Medicine May Be Hard to Swallow," *New York Newsday,* 23 February 1995, p. A41.

97. Julie Defalco, "First Steps for FDA Reform," CEI Update (Washington, D.C.: Competitive Enterprise Institute), December 1997, p. 9.

98. Sam Kazman, op. cit., interview with author.

99. "Safety Last," *Washington Times* (23 December 1997), editorial, p. A14.

100. "A National Survey of Neurologists and Neurosurgeons Regarding the Food and Drug Administration," (Washington, D.C.: Competitive Enterprise Institute, undated report).

101. Thomas G. Donlan, "A Looming Disaster," *Barron's* (12 October 1998), p. 59; "Protecting Patients to Death," *Washington Times* (18 October 1998), editorial, p. B2; "A New FDA Commissar," *Augusta* (Georgia) *Chronicle* (5 December 1998), editorial, p. A4.

102. "CEI Survey Finds Neurologists Favor Greater Access to Off-Label Therapies," *FDA Week,* Vol. 4, no. 42 (16 October 1998), p. 17.

103. Thomas Moore, George Washington University, interview with author.

104. "Anemic Drug Oversight," *Los Angeles Times* (13 December 1998), Part M, p. 4.

105. Ibid.

106. Thomas Moore, op. cit.

CHAPTER 4.

MASKING IDEOLOGY AS RESEARCH:
BRINGING DOWN HEAD START

1. Edward Hudgins, Cato Institute, interview with author.

2. Edward Zigler, "Caveat Emptor: Ideology Passing as Social Science in Head Start" (unpublished paper, Yale University, 1993), p. 3.

3. Helen Blank, Children's Defense Fund, interview with author.
4. Ibid.
5. "End Head Start, Study Urges," Cato Institute press release, 18 December 1992.
6. John Hood, "Caveat Emptor: The Head Start Scam," *Policy Analysis,* No. 187 (Washington, D.C.: Cato Institute, 18 December 1992), p. 11.
7. Ibid., p. 14.
8. Ibid., pp. 1, 2.
9. Zigler, op. cit., p. 2.
10. Hood, op. cit., p. 8.
11. Ibid.
12. Ibid., p. 6.
13. Ibid., p. 6f.
14. Zigler, op. cit., p. 4, also interview with Lisa Sheikh, researcher, Harvard School of Public Health, obtained in connection with a project on science, technology, and the news media.
15. Hood, op. cit., p. 10.
16. Zigler, op. cit., p. 14.
17. Hood, op. cit., p. 10.
18. Ibid., pp. 1, 14.
19. Ibid., p. 14.
20. Ibid., p. 13.
21. Ibid.
22. Ibid.
23. Cato Institute, press release (18 December 1996), op. cit.
24. John Hood, "What's Wrong with Head Start," *Wall Street Journal* (19 February 1993), p. 14.
25. Zigler, op. cit., p. 2.
26. John Hood, interview with Lisa Sheikh.
27. Ibid.
28. Lisa Walker, executive director, Education Writers Association, interview with Lisa Sheikh.

29. Mary Jordan, "As Politicians Expand Head Start, Experts Question Worth, Efficiency," *Washington Post* (19 February 1993), p. A4.
30. Mary Jordan, "Academics, Others Question Effectiveness of Head Start," *Phoenix Gazette* (19 February 1993), p. A2.
31. "Time for a Colder, Closer Look at Head Start," *Macon Telegraph,* editorial (29 February 1993).
32. Bill Johnson, "Claims of Head Start's Success May Be Exaggerated," *Detroit News* (23 April 1993).
33. Bill Johnson, *Detroit News* editorial writer, interview with Lisa Sheikh.
34. Linda Seebach, "Head Start Program Leaves Kids at the Starting Gate," *St. Petersburg Times* (28 February 1993).
35. "Head Start Is Effective," Cathy Ridenour, policy chairperson, Western Maryland Child Care Resource Center, letter in *Baltimore Sun* (28 April 1993).
36. Mary Jordan, *Washington Post,* op. cit.
37. Edward Zigler, professor of psychology, Yale University, interview with author.
38. Ibid.
39. Zigler, op. cit., pp. i, 2.
40. Ibid., p. ii.
41. Zigler, op. cit.
42. Helen Blank, op. cit.
43. Ibid.
44. Sarah Greene, Executive Director, Head Start Association, interview with author.

CHAPTER 5.
ADVANCING A CAUSE: REMAKING MEDICARE

1. Jeff Shear, "The Ax Files," *The National Journal,* Vol. 27, no. 14., 15 April 1994, p. 53.

2. Robyn Stone, speech: "Aging: A Major News Story in the 21st Century," at Symposium, International Leadership Center on Longevity, 18 September 1997.

3. Robert Rosenblatt, comment to Stone speech symposium, "Aging: A Major News Story in the 21st Century," International Leadership Center on Longevity, 18 September 1997.

4. Larry Mone, president, the Manhattan Institute, interview with author.

5. Cheryl Rubin, director of public relations, The Heritage Foundation, interview with author.

6. Bruce Vladeck, former administrator, Health Care Financing Administration, interview with author.

7. David Broder, "With a Little Courage, Clinton Can Make History with Medicare," editorial section, *Austin American-Statesman*, 6 July 1997, p. H3.

8. "Medicare: New Choices New Worries," *Consumer Reports*, September 1998, p. 27.

9. Marilyn Moon, economist, The Urban Institute, interview with author.

10. James Ridgeway, "Heritage on the Hill," *Nation*, 22 December 1997, p. 16.

11. "Structural Reform on Medicare," *Committee Brief: A Special Report to the House Ways and Means Committee* (Washington, D.C.: The Heritage Foundation, 2 February 1995).

12. "Structural Reform of Medicare Proposed," The Heritage Foundation news release (Washington, D.C.: 15 February 1995).

13. "Reform Medicare or Face Huge Tax Increases, Analysis Says," The Heritage Foundation news release (Washington, D.C.: 4 May 1995).

14. Ibid.

15. "The High Cost of Not Reforming Medicare," an F.Y.I. from The Heritage Foundation (Washington, D.C.: 4 May 1995),

and "What It Takes to Reform Medicare," an invitation to a lecture by Rep. William Thomas, 4 May 1995.

16. "Editors' Views—The Budget," *MacNeil / Lehrer NewsHour,* 12 May 1995.

17. Memorandum from Frank Luntz to interested parties (Arlington, Va.: The Luntz Research Companies), 7 June 1995.

18. Ibid.

19. Stuart M. Butler and John S. Barry, "Solving the Problem of Middle-Class Entitlements," in *Mandate for Leadership IV— Turning Ideas into Actions,* edited by Stuart M. Butler and Kim R. Holmes (Washington, D.C.: The Heritage Foundation, 1997, p. 302.

20. Bernard Shaw, "Rep. Dan Miller Gives GOP Perspective on Medicare," *Inside Politics,* CNN (Cable News Network, Inc., 3 May 1995).

21. "Medicare Increases Called Cuts," *MediaNomics,* vol. 3, issue 5, June 1995, p. 2.

22. Ibid.

23. "Mangling the Medicare Math," *MediaWatch,* vol. 9, issue 6, June 1995, p. 1.

24. "Medicare Increases Called Cuts," op. cit., p. 2f.

25. Marilyn Moon, "Restructuring Medicare's Cost-Sharing," The Commonwealth Fund, December 1996, p. 9.

26. Michael Weiskopf and David Maraniss, "Republican Leaders Win Battle by Defining Terms of Combat," *Washington Post,* 29 October 1995, p. A1.

27. "Medicare Reporting Improving, But . . . ," *MediaNomics,* vol. 3, issue 8, September 1995, p. 2.

28. Paul Starobin, "There Are Watchdogs and There Are Watchdogs," *National Journal,* 30 November 1996, p. 2587.

29. *CBS Evening News* transcript, 19 October 1995.

30. "Media vs. a Balanced Budget," *MediaWatch,* vol. 9, issue 11, November 1995, p. 1.

31. *NBC Today* transcript, 24 October 1995.

32. Cheryl Rubin, op. cit.

33. "Heritage Foundation Recommends Major Medicare Reform," The Heritage Foundation news release (Washington, D.C.: 15 February 1995).

34. "What To Do About Medicare," The Heritage Foundation (Washington, D.C.: 26 June 1995).

35. "Heritage Foundation Recommends Overhaul for Medicare Program," *Wall Street Journal,* 27 June 1995, p. C7.

36. Patricia Hill, "Heritage Proposes Seniors Health Plan to Replace Medicare," *Washington Times,* 27 June 1995, p. A8.

37. "'Medichoice'—or Bust," *Rocky Mountain News* editorial, 23 July 1995, p. 93A.

38. "Medichoice for Medicare," (Memphis) *Commercial Appeal,* viewpoint, 23 July 1995, p. 6B.

39. Cal Thomas, "Medicare at 30: The Cost, The Deception and The Cure," *Times-Picayune,* 28 July 1995, p. B7.

40. Cheryl Rubin, op. cit.

41. Cover letter from Mark Trapscott, Senior Writer, The Heritage Foundation, to journalists, 8 August 1995; John C. Liu, "A Guide to Medicare Reform Proposals," *F.Y.I.* (Washington, D.C.: The Heritage Foundation, 4 August 1995); and Stuart M. Butler, "Comparing Apples with Apples on Medicare," *F.Y.I.* (Washington, D.C.: The Heritage Foundation, 4 August 1995).

42. Robert E. Moffit, John C. Liu, and David H. Winston, "What Americans Will Pay If Congress Fails to Reform Medicare: The State and Congressional District Impact," *F.Y.I.* (Washington, D.C.: The Heritage Foundation, 19 September 1995).

43. "Two Cheers for the House Medicare Plan," *Executive Memorandum* (Washington, D.C.: The Heritage Foundation, 22 September 1995).

44. "Federal Health Program Success Is Lesson for Medicare Reformers, Analyst Says," The Heritage Foundation news release, 25 September 1995; "FEHBP Controls Costs Again: More Lessons for Medicare Reformers," *F.Y.I.* (Washington, D.C.: The Heritage Foundation, 25 September 1995).

45. Cover letter from Wanda Moebius, The Heritage Foundation, to journalists, 28 September 1995, and John C. Liu and Robert E. Moffit, "A Taxpayer's Guide to the Medicare Crisis," *Heritage Talking Points* (Washington, D.C.: The Heritage Foundation, 27 September 1995).

46. Cover letter from Sam Walker, The Heritage Foundation, to editors, 6 October 1995, and "Cutting Red Tape on Clinical Labs: Why Congress Should Deregulate Doctors" (Washington, D.C.: The Heritage Foundation, 27 September 1995).

47. Cover letter from Sam Walker, The Heritage Foundation, to journalists, 12 October 1995; Rep. Dan Miller, "Medicare Miracles," *Point of View* (Washington, D.C.: The Heritage Foundation, 12 October 1995); and "What's Really at Stake in the Medicare Debate," *Point of View* (Washington, D.C.: The Heritage Foundation, 12 October 1995).

48. Ibid.

49. "Without Reform, Medicare Will Cost $123 Billion More per Year, Analysts Say," The Heritage Foundation news release, 16 October 1995, and David H. Winston, Christine L. Olson, and Rea S. Herderman, "The Cost of No Medicare Reform: What Industry and Government Would Pass On to Consumers, Investors, Taxpayers, and Workers," *F.Y.I.* (Washington, D.C.: The Heritage Foundation, 16 October 1995).

50. "Private Sector Offers Lessons for Medicare Reform, Analyst Says," The Heritage Foundation news release, 31 October 1995.

51. Cover letter from Weldon Freeman, The Heritage Foundation, to journalists, 14 November 1995.

52. Cover letter from Sam Walker, The Heritage Foundation, to journalists, 16 November 1995.

53. "Bridging the Budget Gap on Medicare," *F.Y.I.* (Washington, D.C.: The Heritage Foundation), 21 November 1995.

54. Rep. Martin R. Hoke, "Big GOP Push for Medicare," *Cleveland Plain Dealer,* 19 October 1995, editorials and forum section, p. 11B.

55. Stuart Butler, "Old Plan Can Remedy Health-Care Crisis," *Newsday,* 17 September 1995, p. A40.

56. Stuart Butler, "'Cutting' Medicare Isn't Enough," *Dayton Daily News,* 20 August 1995, op-ed, p. 9B.

57. "Medicare Reform," *MacNeil / Lehrer NewsHour,* 19 October 1995.

58. Ed Rothschild, communications director, Citizen Action, interview with author.

59. Judith Haveman and Spencer Rich, "Wording of House GOP's Medicare Memo Upsets Senior Citizen Groups," *Washington Post,* 23 July 1995, p. A10.

60. Weiskopf and Maraniss, *Washington Post,* op. cit.

61. Rex Nelson, "Building a Conservative Juggernaut: First GOP-Led Congress in Decades Gives Think Tank Power to Shape Laws," *Arkansas Democrat Gazette,* 5 November 1995, p. 1A.

62. Robert Dreyfuss, "Neighbor to Neighbor Takes On Medicare Myths," *Extra,* March/April 1997, p. 17.

63. *Mandate for Leadership IV,* op. cit., p. 301.

64. Ibid., p. 310f.

65. Ibid., p. 306.

66. Robert Pear, "House Panel Votes Changes to Try to Keep Medicare Solvent," *New York Times,* 10 June 1997, p. D25.

67. Robert Pear, "Seeking Bipartisan Support, Republicans Offer Medicare Plan," *New York Times,* 4 June 1997, p. A20.

68. "Clinton Budget 'Not Serious' About Medicare Crisis, Ana-

lysts Say," The Heritage Foundation news release, 27 February 1997.

69. Cover letter from Randy Clerihue, The Heritage Foundation, to journalists, and *Balancing America's Budget: Ending the Era of Big Government* (Washington, D.C.: The Heritage Foundation), undated.

70. "Time Is Running Out for Medicare Reform," *Backgrounder* (Washington, D.C.: The Heritage Foundation), 30 April 1997.

71. "Budget Cuts Alone Will Not Save Medicare, Analyst Says," The Heritage Foundation news release, 6 May 1997.

72. "Budget Deal Contains Meager Tax Relief, Huge Spending Increases, Analysis Finds," The Heritage Foundation news release, 9 May 1997.

73. Cover letter from Sam Walker, The Heritage Foundation, to journalists, 12 May 1997, and "The Budget Deal's Medicare Benefit Inflation," *Backgrounder* (Washington, D.C.: The Heritage Foundation), 12 May 1997.

74. Cover letter from Sam Walker, The Heritage Foundation, to journalists, 5 June 1997.

75. Cover letter from Randy Clerihue, The Heritage Foundation, to journalists, 12 June 1997.

76. Cover letter from Andrew B. Campbell, The Heritage Foundation, to journalists, 16 June 1997.

77. Cover letter from Sam Walker, The Heritage Foundation, to journalists, 27 June 1997.

78. "Will Anyone Dare Touch Medicare?" *The Economist,* 28 June 1997, p. 25.

79. Cover letter from Sam Walker, The Heritage Foundation, to journalists, 11 July 1997, and Carrie J. Gavora, "How to Reform Medicare: A Reconciliation Checklist," *Issue Bulletin* (Washington, D.C.: The Heritage Foundation), 11 July 1997.

80. Cover letter from Cheryl Rubin, The Heritage Foundation, to journalists, 5 August 1997.

81. "Sickening Waste," *Orange County Register,* 18 July 1997, editorial.

82. *Mandate for Leadership IV,* op. cit., p. 305.

83. Ibid., p. 305f.

84. "Medicare—Preparing for the Challenge of the 21st Century," co-editors Robert D. Reischaur and Judith Lave, Proceedings of National Academy of Social Insurance 23, 24 January 1997, p. 278.

85. "United Seniors Offer Medicare Reform Proposal," United Seniors Association press release by Hugh C. Newton and Associates, Alexandria, Va., July 1996.

86. Solicitation from United Seniors Association.

87. Steven Findlay, "Elderly Call Medicare Rule Unfair," *USA Today,* 26 November 1997, p. 6A.

88. Cover letter from John Raughter, The Heritage Foundation, to journalists, 4 August 1997.

89. Press release, The Kaiser-Harvard Program on the Public and Health and Health/Social Policy, 20 October 1998.

90. "Making the Budget Bearable," *New York Times,* editorial, 7 February 1997, p. 32.

91. Cover letter to journalists, The Heritage Foundation, 26 January 1999.

92. News release, The Heritage Foundation, 17 March 1999.

CONCLUSION: THE RIGHT WING'S SUCCESS

1. David Callahan, "$1 Billion for Ideas: Conservative Think Tanks in the 1990s" (Washington, D.C.: National Committee for Responsive Philanthropy, March 1999), p. 36.

2. Dan Mitchell, senior fellow, The Heritage Foundation, interview with author.

3. John Rother, chief lobbyist, American Association of Retired Persons, interview with author.

4. S. Robert Lichter, "Consistently Liberal: But Does it Matter?" *Forbes* media critic, Fall 1996, p. 30.

5. Ibid., p. 32.

6. David Croteau, "Examining the 'Liberal Media' Claim," *A FAIR Report,* June 1998, <http://www.fair.org/reports/journalists-survey.html> (7 April 1999).

7. Ibid.

8. James Warren, Washington bureau chief, *Chicago Tribune,* interview with author.

9. The Times Mirror Center for The People & The Press, *The People, The Press and Their Leaders* (Washington, D.C.: The Times Mirror Company, 1995), p. 13f.

10. William W. Beach and Gareth G. Davis, *Social Security's Rate of Return,* A Report of the Heritage Center for Data Analysis (Washington, D.C.: The Heritage Foundation), 15 January 1998.

11. John Mueller, "Winners and Losers from Privatizing Social Security," The National Committee to Preserve Social Security and Medicare, 1999.

12. William W. Beach and Gareth G. Davis, *Social Security's Rate of Return, A Reply to Our Critics,* A Report of the Heritage Center for Data Analysis (Washington, D.C.: The Heritage Foundation, December 14, 1998).

13. Elizabeth Lesly Stevens, "Mouse.ke.fear," *Brill's Content,* December 1998/January 1999, p. 95.

14. Jay Harris, publisher, *Mother Jones,* at lecture series, "Self-Censorship and the Media, What the Press Doesn't Report and Why," New York University, 21 April 1999.

15. Jay Harris, publisher, *Mother Jones,* interview with author.

16. Eric Engberg, CBS correspondent, interview with author.

17. Glen Totten, Totten Communications, interview with author.

18. William Serrin, professor of journalism, New York University, interview with author.

19. Michael Pertschuk, co-director, The Advocacy Institute, interview with author.

20. David Callahan, "$1 Billion for Ideas: Conservative Think Tanks in the 1990s," a report from the National Committee for Responsive Philanthropy, March 1999, p. 37.

21. Michael H. Shuman, "Why Do Progressive Foundations Give Too Little to Too Many," *The Nation,* 12 January 1998, p. 11.

22. Michael Pertschuk, op. cit.

23. Walker Lundy, editor, St. Paul Pioneer Press, interview with author.

24. Glen Totten, op. cit.

25. *Striking the Balance: Audience Interest, Business Pressure and Journalists' Values* (Washington, D.C.: The Pew Research Center for the People & The Press, in association with Committee of Concerned Journalists, undated), p. 3.

26. Ibid.

27. Walker Lundy, op. cit.

28. Gregg Easterbrook, interview with author.

29. James Carey, "Journalists Just Leave: The Ethics of an Anomalous Profession," in *The Media & Morality,* edited by Robert M. Baird, William E. Loges, and Stuart E. Rosenbaum (Amherst, New York: Prometheus Books, 1999), p. 51.

Index

197